Published by Wisconsin Trails Magazine, a division of
Wisconsin Tales and Trails, Inc., P.O. Box 5650, Madison,
Wisconsin 53705.

Library of Congress 88–51259
Library of Congress Cataloging in Publication Data applied for
ISBN 0–915024–33–0

EDITOR: Geri Nixon
FOOD STYLIST: Suzanne Breckenridge
BOOK DESIGN: Deb Gallagher
TYPESETTING: KC Graphics, Madison
PRINTING: Litho Productions, Inc., Madison

Printed in U.S.A.

First Printing 1988

INTRODUCTION

From the bounty of early spring crops to late autumn harvests, Wisconsin is bursting with good things to eat. It is this great variety and abundance of locally grown fresh food that inspires the cooking of "Country Gourmet" food column authors Marge Synder and Suzanne Breckenridge. Since 1981 this culinary team has demonstrated to *Wisconsin Trails* magazine readers how to make every menu a grand one using the finest and freshest Wisconsin products.

Now in *Wisconsin Country Gourmet* they have brought the best of these columns together. Here is a cookbook for all seasons and occasions, filled with recipes, menus and ideas that celebrate the bounty of this great state—its fresh garden produce, orchard crops, crops in the wild, catches from rivers and lakes, domestic livestock and abundant wild game.

Wisconsin Country Gourmet is a unique regional cookbook. With a wealth of ethnic populations—German, Scandinavian, Italian, Yugoslavian, Greek, Polish, and many others—Wisconsin regional cooking is frequently ethnic cooking. On these pages you'll find pierogi, dolmades, tortellini next to such popular all-American fare as chicken on the grill or cherry pie.

We invite you to enjoy a taste of Wisconsin, inspired by the seasons. This is cooking at its finest—fresh, regional ingredients and a mingling of the culinary traditions of the many great people of this state.

—Geri Nixon
Managing Editor, *Wisconsin Trails*

SPRING

SUMMER

AUTUMN

WINTER

SPRING

Surely nothing surpasses in fleeting perfection the Wisconsin spring, which comes not by the calendar but according to the whims of our Midwestern weather—unfolding leisurely with the south wind one year, moving north in gentle waves from Beloit to Bayfield, another year coming in a sudden rush appearing briefly between an extended winter and an early summer. With it comes the joyously anticipated spring harvest. Whether hunting the woods for the elusive morel, casting for fish in your favorite lake or stream, harvesting your own patch of greens or asparagus, or simply shopping the early farmers markets, the bounty of spring is everywhere. For the country gourmet it's an exciting time, when menus turn toward the fresh produce of the season and renewed culinary creativity abounds.

GOURMET DAIRY DISHES

It only takes a short drive through Wisconsin's countryside in summer to understand our state's distinction as America's Dairyland. Carefully tended farmlands, herds of well-fed cattle, hilly lush pastures, and an occasional cheese factory dot the landscape. We owe these picturesque scenes and our national title to the thousands of small, independent dairy farmers who make Wisconsin the leader in milk production.

Wisconsin has celebrated June as "Dairy Month" since 1936. Throughout the state, counties set up elaborate exhibits, demonstrations, concession stands, farm tours, product samples, festivals, old-fashioned milking contests and forums to promote Wisconsin's dairy industry.

Although age, activity level or dietary requirement may dictate the form, dairy products fit into nearly everyone's daily nourishment. One of the milk products closely linked to the calorie-conscious is cottage cheese. This soft, unripened cheese is made from strained and seasoned curds of skim milk. Similar unripened varieties are Farmer's cheese, or pot cheese (drier and solidly packed), hoop cheese (pressed, lightly cured, dried and coated with wax), ricotta cheese (less sodium than cottage cheese, but more perishable), cream cheese and its low-fat counterpart, Neufchatel.

With its slightly acid taste, buttermilk reigns more as a creative addition to cooking than as a beverage. It makes light and fluffy cakes, muffins, biscuits and pancakes, and adds zest to cold soups, vegetable dips and salad dressings. For old-fashioned, tender, juicy fried chicken simply dip pieces in buttermilk, roll in seasoned flour and fry.

While yogurt's fame as a healthy snack food is well established, its tart flavor also makes it a refreshing substitute in recipes calling for sour cream—quiches, stroganoffs, omelets, baked potatoes, salad dressings, pancakes, waffles, muffins and ready-to-eat cereals. For some, though, it will never be a substitute for rich and smooth sour cream, made from fresh cream that's heated with souring agents. Its combination tart / sweet taste makes it adaptable to a wide range of foods—from baked potatoes to cheesecakes, salad dressings, sauces, dips and as a quick dessert mixed with a seasonal fruit.

Among all dairy products few can compare to the taste and versatility of *real* cream—high in calories, high in fat, high in everything including taste. The gourmet or heavy variety is ideal for cooking over high heat, great for sauces, as it neither curdles or lumps. The ultra-pasteurized varieties—half-and-half and whipping cream—have a long shelf-life (60–90 days under refrigeration) but are not recommended for high-temperature cooking.

In their infinite variety, dairy products play a large role in every cook's creations and in the state's industry. Among them, perhaps none says "Wisconsin" better than cheese. You'll find a complete section on this product under "Winter."

Dairy-good desserts from the oven—almond-raisin blintzes and chocolate cheesecake.

COLD CUCUMBER SOUP

The wonderful flavor of dill is brought out in this refreshing, simple soup. Be sure to include it in your menu for the next family picnic or barbeque—even the kids will love it.

5 cucumbers, peeled and seeded

½ cup fresh parsley, chopped

6 scallions or green onions

2 tablespoons fresh dill

¼ cup fresh lemon juice

1 quart buttermilk

1 pint sour cream

salt and pepper

Sprinkle cucumbers with salt and let stand 30 minutes; drain. Place cucumbers in a food processor or blender along with parsley, scallions, dill, lemon juice and buttermilk. Whirl until very smooth; taste and adjust seasonings. Stir in sour cream and chill 4 hours or more. Garnish with additional minced, peeled cucumbers.

Serves 6

CHICKEN BREASTS IN CHAMPAGNE SAUCE

A very elegant, rich dinner entree that's surprisingly simple to prepare—a sure winner at your next dinner party.

2 whole chicken breasts, halved, skinned and boned

salt and pepper

1 tablespoon minced fresh parsley

2 tablespoons minced fresh tarragon or

3 teaspoons dried tarragon

3 tablespoons butter

1 minced shallot or 2 tablespoons minced green onions

⅔ cup champagne or dry white wine

½ cup heavy cream

1 teaspoon minced lemon peel, julienned

Beurre Manié (2 teaspoons each of flour and butter, kneaded together)

Sprinkle the chicken with salt and pepper and coat with the minced parsley and tarragon (can be covered in plastic wrap and refrigerated for several hours). Melt 3 tablespoons butter over low heat and sauté chicken, cover. Cook for 10 minutes or until it is opaque and just cooked. Transfer to a heated platter and keep warm.

Sauté the shallot or green onions in butter remaining in the pan, until softened. Add the champagne or wine and bring to a boil; scrape pan. Reduce liquid to 3 tablespoons, simmer 5–7 minutes. Stir in cream and bring to a boil, simmer 3 minutes. Add the lemon peel and whisk in the Beurre Manié, simmer until smooth and slightly thickened. Adjust the seasonings, add more lemon peel or tarragon if needed. Pour sauce over warmed chicken.

Serves 4

FRUIT SALAD WITH YOGURT-MINT DRESSING

The sweet-tart taste of this salad teams beautifully with Indian curries, spicy Mexican dishes and Cajun foods.

1 8-ounce carton plain yogurt

2 tablespoons honey

1 teaspoon grated orange rind

½ teaspoon grated fresh ginger root

2–3 tablespoons minced fresh mint or

2 teaspoons dried mint

6–8 cups assorted sliced and cut up fruit (strawberries, blueberries, melons, pineapples, grapes, cherries, etc.)

lettuce leaves

Combine yogurt, honey, orange rind, ginger root and mint; mix well. Chill several hours. Toss with fruit just before serving and place lettuce on each plate or on a platter.

Serves 4

GREEN GODDESS SALAD DRESSING

A zesty, piquant dressing for salads with assertive greens—chicory, endive, escarole, romaine. A pleasant addition to your own salad bar.

1 egg yolk

1 tablespoon white wine vinegar

1½ teaspoons lemon juice

¼ teaspoon salt

1 teaspoon each dried tarragon and Dijon-style mustard

6–8 anchovy fillets, chopped

1 small clove garlic, chopped

2 green onions, chopped

½ cup minced fresh parsley

¼ cup minced watercress

⅓ cup each olive oil and salad oil

½ cup sour cream

In a food processor or blender combine egg yolk, vinegar, lemon juice, salt, tarragon, mustard, anchovies, garlic, green onions, parsley and watercress; blend smooth. At low speed, add olive oil and salad oil, whirl until thick. Pour into a bowl and mix in sour cream. Chill several hours before using.

Makes 1 cup

ALMOND-RAISIN BLINTZES

Perfect for lunch or brunch and can be made ahead and reheated.

FILLING

2 cups small-curd cottage cheese, drained

1 egg, slightly beaten

½ cup raisins or currants

½ teaspoon almond extract

2 tablespoons sugar

½ cup toasted sliced almonds

butter

powdered sugar

sour cream

Combine cottage cheese, egg, raisins or currants, almond extract, sugar and ⅓ cup almonds in a bowl; mix well and set aside.

To assemble, place 1–2 tablespoons filling in center of each crepe and fold in edges like a square. Cover with plastic wrap and refrigerate overnight.

Just before serving, sauté blintzes in butter, fold-side down, until heated through and slightly browned. Serve with powdered sugar or a dollop of sour cream and a sprinkling of toasted almonds.

CREPES

⅞ cup flour

⅛ teaspoon salt

3 eggs

2 tablespoons melted butter, cooled

1½ cups milk

Combine in blender and whip for 30 seconds. Scrape and blend for 30 seconds more. Cover and chill for 1 hour.

To make crepes, heat 1 tablespoon oil in crepe or omelet pan or in heavy 5- to 6-inch skillet; pour out oil. (Or place pan over medium heat; brush with oil.) Lift pan from heat; pour in just enough batter to cover bottom. Swirl pan so batter completely covers bottom in very thin layer. Return to medium heat; cook until crepe is set and edges dry. Slide spatula under edge of crepe to loosen. Lift carefully; turn gently. Brown other side just a few seconds; remove from heat. Shake pan to loosen; slide crepe from pan onto oiled waxed paper. Cook crepes until all batter is used. Separate with waxed paper oiled on both sides.

Makes 14 blintzes

CHOCOLATE CHEESECAKE WITH RASPBERRY SAUCE

Make this super rich cheesecake one day ahead and decorate with fresh raspberries just before serving.

1¼ cups graham cracker crumbs

1½ cups plus 1 tablespoon sugar, divided

4 tablespoons butter, melted

18 ounces semi-sweet chocolate

¾ cup extra strong hot coffee with 1 tablespoon dry coffee granular added (preferably espresso)

24 ounces cream cheese, softened

6 eggs

3 tablespoons vanilla

RASPBERRY SAUCE

2 cups raspberries

¾ cup sugar

1 teaspoon arrowroot or cornstarch mixed with ¼ cup water

1 tablespoon fresh lemon juice

¼ cup kirsch

Butter sides of 10-inch springform pan. Combine graham cracker crumbs, 1 tablespoon sugar and butter. Mix well and press onto bottom of prepared pan. Melt chocolate with the coffee in the top of a double boiler. Beat cream cheese until light and creamy. Gradually add in the remaining 1½ cups of sugar. Add eggs, one at a time, beating well after each addition. Beat in vanilla. Add chocolate mixture, mix until blended.

Pour into prepared springform. Bake in a preheated 350 degree oven for 50 minutes. Turn off heat, open oven door and let cake cool 2 to 3 hours in oven.

While the cake cools, purée the raspberries in a food processor or blender; whirl until smooth. Sieve raspberries removing seeds. Place purée in a small saucepan, add sugar and cornstarch mixture, simmer until thick. Remove from heat, add lemon juice and kirsch, serve with cheesecake.

Serves 14

Hearty fare from Serbia

FOOD FULL OF GUSTO

There are some meals that satisfy the spirit as much as the appetite. Such is the case with Serbian food. Coming from the large eastern region of Yugoslavia, the Serbs are influenced in their cooking by Romania, Bulgaria, Hungary and the Middle East. Meat and fish stews, grilled foods and hearty vegetable casseroles are standard Serbian fare, and accompanied by fresh fruit, cheeses, hearty country breads, nuts and plum brandy, they are part of an earthy and satisfying meal.

Wisconsin is home to many people of Serbian ancestry, particularly in the Milwaukee area. Through the generations strong traditions have remained, especially religious ones, such as the celebration of *Slava* (a family's patron saint's day.) On this day friends and relatives are invited to share in a festive dinner. *Patron Saint Cake* is served (every family has a treasured recipe) and a bowl of cooked wheat sweetened with honey, *koljivo,* is offered, symbolizing the nativity and life.

The Serbs are masters at turning simple ingredients into spicy, strong-flavored dishes. For example, *sarma,* or cabbage rolls, are almost a staple in their diet. Unlike most cabbage rolls, this dish is made with soured whole cabbage leaves, sauerkraut, ground meats and smoked ham. It's included in every Serbian holiday menu and tastes even better the next day.

Like other Eastern Europeans, the Serbians make legendary filled strudel dishes. Stretched so fine you can almost read through it, the paper-thin pastry is filled and rolled with assorted nuts,

spices, cheeses, fruits and honey. The dough is also used in making a tasty main dish, *burek,* which is filled with ground meats or cheese.

Along with the strudels, the Serbians' dessert menu extends to tortes, cakes and cookies, all made with only the freshest cream, butter and eggs. One of the sweetest foods is *slatko,* a thick preserve, usually made from plums. In it, the fruit is mixed with sugar and cooked slowly until a syrup forms but the fruit still holds its shape. It can be used as a dessert filling, but more often a spoonful of it, along with a glass of water is offered to visitors as a sign of hospitality. No report on Serbian customs would be complete without mentioning the national beverage, *slivovitz,* plum brandy. Yugoslavia grows more plum trees than any other country in the world, and puts the harvest to good use by turning those purple delights into many varieties of brandy. The potent slivovitz is served anytime Serbians celebrate—with snacks or desserts, after dinner, at parties or simply mixed with tea on cold winter nights.

"Na zdravlje" (to your health).

Chicken in garlic sauce tastes even better with Serbia's national beverage, plum brandy or slivovitz.

EGGPLANT CAVIAR
(Srpski Ajvar)

We often serve appetizers with an international flavor: this is one of our favorites. Try it with slices of dark bread, feta cheese, roasted peppers and an assortment of imported beers.

1½ pounds eggplant

4 large green peppers

1 teaspoon salt

freshly ground pepper

½ teaspoon garlic, finely minced

2 tablespoons fresh lemon juice

6 tablespoons olive oil

2 tablespoons parsley, minced

Place eggplant and green peppers on cookie sheet in a preheated 500 degree oven. Bake peppers 25 minutes, remove. Bake eggplant 15–20 minutes longer or until tender. Wrap in a damp towel and let stand 10 minutes to loosen skin.

Peel the peppers, discard seeds and ribs, slice in thin strips and transfer to a bowl. Peel the eggplant, chop and squeeze dry in a towel. Add to peppers. Add salt, pepper, garlic, lemon juice and olive oil. Taste and adjust. Chill and sprinkle with parsley.

CHICKEN IN GARLIC SAUCE
(Pile u sosu od be Log Kuka)

A creamy garlic-sage sauce makes this chicken dish spicy and aromatic. Serve with noodles or steamed new potatoes.

1 frying chicken, cut up in serving pieces

1 teaspoon salt

⅓ cup flour

2 teaspoons sage, cut up or crumbled

vegetable oil

3 cloves garlic, chopped finely

3 tablespoons flour

1 tablespoon vinegar

½ cup light cream

In a 3-quart pan poach the chicken with just enough water to cover, add the salt and simmer in covered pan until almost done. Remove chicken and drain, reserving the broth.

In a bowl combine the flour and sage; season with salt and freshly ground pepper if desired. Roll chicken in flour mixture, coating lightly.

Heat vegetable oil in a heavy skillet and fry the chicken until browned lightly. Remove chicken and keep warm. Pour off excess oil if it's more than 3 tablespoons. In the skillet add garlic and cook about 2 minutes. Do not brown. Add the 3 tablespoons flour and brown. Pour reserved broth gradually into flour mixture whisking until smooth. Season to taste, add vinegar and cook while whisking about 3 minutes until thick and smooth. Add the cream and combine well, then heat and pour over warm chicken.

Serves 4–6

LAMB AND VEGETABLE CASSEROLE
(Djuvec)

We find this casserole improves in flavor when made ahead and reheated. Serve it with a robust green salad, dark bread and red wine.

4 slices bacon, diced

3 medium onions, sliced

½ teaspoon minced garlic

3 pounds meat (combination of lamb and pork, cut in 1½ inch cubes)

1–28 ounce can peeled tomatoes, drained and sliced

1 medium eggplant, peeled and cubed

2 zucchini, sliced

4 green peppers, sliced

1 cup green beans, sliced

4 large potatoes, peeled and sliced ¼ inch thick (or substitute 1 cup uncooked rice)

1 bay leaf

salt and pepper

¼ cup beef stock

Cook bacon in large ovenproof casserole. Remove and sauté onions and garlic. Remove and brown meat. Combine with bacon and onion mixture. Arrange half of the meat mixture in the bottom of the casserole. Add half the vegetables, and repeat. Place bay leaf on top. Season, add stock and cover. Bake at 350 for 1½ hours or until tender. Uncover during last 30 minutes to evaporate some of the liquid.

Serves 8–10

BRAISED CARROTS WITH YOGURT

Don't let the simplicity of this carrot recipe fool you—it's very spicy with a hint of dill and teams perfectly with grilled poultry or shish-kebabs.

¼ cup butter

8 medium carrots, peeled and cut into ¼ inch rounds

½ cup sliced scallions

1 teaspoon sugar

⅛–¼ teaspoon cayenne pepper

salt and freshly ground pepper

1 cup plain yogurt

2 tablespoons fresh dill, chopped

In a heavy saucepan, melt butter. Add carrots, scallions and sugar. Cover and braise until tender, 5–10 minutes, being careful not to burn them. When done, season with cayenne, salt and pepper. Combine yogurt and dill and stir into carrot mixture. Serve immediately.

Serves 4–6

NUT SQUARES
(Cheturtasti Kolaci sa Orasima)

A perfect potluck dessert—easy to make, spicy and light with the zest of apricots.

½ cup butter

⅓ cup sugar

1½ cups sifted flour

3 egg yolks

1 teaspoon lemon juice

½ teaspoon grated lemon rind

1 egg white, slightly beaten

⅔ cup apricot preserve

6 eggs, separated

½ cup sugar

2 cups ground walnuts

2 tablespoons flour

1 teaspoon vanilla

In a large bowl combine the butter, ⅓ cup sugar, 1½ cups flour, 3 egg yolks, lemon juice and rind. Turn out on a lightly floured surface and knead until dough holds together. With a rolling pin, roll dough to fit a 9 × 12 baking pan or dish. Brush with egg white. Bake in a pre-heated 375 degree oven for 10 minutes. Remove from oven and cool.

Spread a layer of apricot preserve. Beat the 6 egg yolks and sugar. Stir in walnuts, flour and vanilla. Beat egg whites until stiff, fold into walnut mixture, spread over dough. Return to the oven, bake at 375 degrees for 15 minutes or until the meringue is brown.

Serves 20–24

SERBIAN APPLE PITA
(Lenja Pita sa Jabukama)

Similar to the traditional apple pie but with a distinctive Serbian crust. Cut in squares, sprinkle with ground nuts and powdered sugar.

½ pound sweet butter

2¾ cups flour

3 tablespoons sugar

3 egg yolks

3 tablespoons sour cream

12–14 medium-sized apples, peeled and sliced thin

2 tablespoons lemon juice

¾ cup sugar

½ teaspoon cinnamon

½ teaspoon nutmeg

3 tablespoons ground walnuts

In a large bowl, blend the butter and flour with a pastry blender. Add the 3 table-spoons sugar, egg yolks and sour cream; make into a dough. Divide into two parts, one slightly larger. Roll larger dough to fit a 9 × 12 baking pan—including sides.

Place apples in a large bowl, add lemon, remaining sugar, cinnamon and nutmeg, and toss until apples are well coated. Place apples in prepared pan. Roll out remaining dough and cover. Seal edges like a pie. Prick with a fork or tooth-pick. Sprinkle with ground nuts. Bake in moderate oven 350–450 degrees for 45 minutes. Sprinkle with powdered sugar before serving.

Serves 18–20

ASPARAGUS

Among the most welcome signs of spring are tender green shoots of asparagus, poking through the soft, warming earth. The name is Greek in origin and refers to all tender shoots picked and eaten while very young. While green asparagus dominates in this country there are also white and purple varieties. White asparagus is prized in Europe and is favored by chefs for its delicate flavor and tenderness. Grown in deep trenches, the stalks are completely covered by dirt to keep them out of the sunlight which would turn them green. Some white asparagus is grown in California for the canning industry and restaurants; very little is shipped elsewhere. Purple asparagus is Italy's choice, preferred for its robust and earthy taste.

A native plant of Europe, asparagus was brought to this country by early settlers who only served the bounty for special guests and special occasions. Europeans still celebrate its harvest with festivals. In Germany, there's *Spargelzeit,* a time when restaurants give asparagus top billing on their menus. France even supports an asparagus museum (in Argenteuil) and an asparagus society (Confrerie de l'Asperge).

It is easy enough to grow your own in Wisconsin. Asparagus is a perennial and once the "bed" is established, you'll be harvesting it for decades with very little maintenance. Select rust-resistant one-year-old roots and plant them in deep trenches. Don't expect dinner the first year, it takes two or more years for a bed to produce enough for a serving.

Eat asparagus as close to picking as possible. Like corn, it contains sugar that turns to starch rapidly. Store spears in the refrigerator wrapped in damp paper towels in a plastic bag or stand them upright in water for not more than four days.

In groceries or at farmers' markets, select firm asparagus of uniform size, with smooth, straight, green stalks. The tips should be compact and tightly closed —no flowering. Some asparagus eaters consider the thicker stalks that come from mature plants to be tastier and more tender than the pencil-thin variety; the most important thing is that they are of uniform size for uniform cooking.

Wash asparagus under cold, running water then break off stalks as far down as they will snap off easily, peeling the larger stalks if they are not of uniform size. Bring one cup of lightly salted water or stock to a boil in a twelve-inch skillet. Place the trimmed asparagus in the pan, cover and lower the heat to medium. Cook until barely tender, five to seven minutes, depending on the thickness of the stalks. They should be slightly crisp; overcooking makes asparagus limp, stringy and strong tasting.

Serve asparagus hot, cold or at room temperature, as a first course, with assorted butters (*beurre blanc,* hollandaise mustard or vinaigrette); as accompaniment to any entree; in salads and pasta sauces; or in soufflés, gratins and casseroles for lunches or light dinners.

Potato salad with a difference—

asparagus adds the crunch

and zest.

TUSCAN SPRING SALAD

Great for picnics and cold buffets, and as an accompaniment to ham, roast beef or barbecued chicken.

10–12 small red potatoes, unpeeled
1 pound fresh asparagus, sliced in 1½–2-inch lengths
5–6 carrots, thinly sliced
¾ cup oil
6 tablespoons red wine vinegar
1 tablespoon sugar
¼ cup minced fresh parsley
1 tablespoon dried basil
2 cloves garlic, minced
salt and freshly ground pepper
2 tablespoons minced shallots or scallions

Cook potatoes in salted water 15–20 minutes or until just tender; drain and set aside. Steam asparagus until barely tender, 1–2 minutes; drain and set aside. Cook carrots 5 minutes, until just tender; drain and set aside. Place all vegetables in a large bowl and chill.

In a blender, combine oil, vinegar, sugar, parsley, basil and garlic; whirl until smooth. Taste and add salt and pepper. Add shallots or scallions and pour over vegetables; toss gently. Taste and add more vinegar, sugar, salt or pepper if needed. Cover and chill. Serve cold or at room temperature on a bed of lettuce.

Serves 4–6

ASPARAGUS ORIENTAL

A versatile dish that's delicious as a salad with chicken or fish, or as an appetizer.

2 tablespoons oil
2 tablespoons sesame seeds
1–1½ pounds fresh asparagus, cut in 1½–2-inch lengths
3 tablespoons vinegar
3 tablespoons sugar
1 teaspoon soy sauce

Heat oil and brown sesame seeds; watch carefully to avoid burning. Remove and let stand 2–3 minutes. Place asparagus in a deep bowl. Pour in oil and seed mixture. Add rest of ingredients; toss carefully. Cover with plastic wrap and refrigerate overnight. Serve in a bowl or drain and place on a bed of lettuce.

Serves 4

ASPARAGUS VINAIGRETTE

Try this zesty spring salad with hot pasta dishes, garlic bread, and a fresh fruit tart.

1 pound asparagus, trimmed
1 large head leaf lettuce, red, green or Boston
½ cup oil, combination olive and vegetable
¼ cup vinegar, raspberry, fruit or herb
1 tablespoon fresh lemon juice
pinch of sugar
1 teaspoon Dijon mustard
½ teaspoon dried tarragon, crumbled
salt and freshly ground pepper
1 small red onion, sliced very thin
1 cup thinly shredded fresh Parmesan cheese (loosely packed)

In a large sauté pan, bring salted water to a boil; add asparagus; blanch about 2–3 minutes until tender crisp. Rinse in cold water and set aside. Wash lettuce, spin dry and line salad plates with leaves; keep cool.

In a jar or blender combine oil, vinegar, lemon juice, sugar, mustard and tarragon; add salt and pepper to taste. Cut asparagus into 2-inch lengths and marinate in vinaigrette about 5 minutes (not more than 15 minutes or asparagus will discolor). Place marinated asparagus over lettuce; lay a few onion rings on top; drizzle with remaining vinaigrette; sprinkle with grated Parmesan and serve.

Serves 6–8

CREAMY BAKED ASPARAGUS

An elegant addition to a spring brunch; serve it with mustard-glazed baked ham, hot muffins and minted fresh fruit salad.

¼ cup minced onion

3 tablespoons butter

¾ pound fresh asparagus, cut in 2-inch pieces

½ teaspoon sugar

salt and freshly ground pepper

2 tablespoons water

6 eggs

⅓ cup heavy cream

¼ teaspoon dried tarragon

1 cup grated Muenster or Swiss cheese

In a skillet, sauté onions in 2 tablespoons butter until soft. Add asparagus, sugar and dash of salt, toss 1 minute. Add 2 tablespoons water; cover and steam 1–2 minutes. Remove cover and evaporate liquid over high heat.

Beat eggs, cream, salt, pepper and tarragon. Melt 1 tablespoon butter in a 9″×9″ or 10″×10″ pan. Pour in egg mixture; sprinkle asparagus evenly over top. Place in a preheated 425 degree oven and bake 5 minutes. Remove and sprinkle cheese on top. Bake 10–12 minutes more, or until golden and puffy. Let stand 5 minutes, then serve in wedges.

Serves 6–8

ASPARAGUS, HAM AND CHICKEN

A delightful brunch, lunch or light dinner dish. Remember not to cook the asparagus too long; you always want tender, crisp stalks.

30 asparagus spears, trimmed to 6 inches and peeled if thick

6 chicken breasts, boned and skinned

6 tablespoons butter

4 tablespoons fresh lemon juice

1 teaspoon dried tarragon

salt and freshly ground pepper

9 slices firm-textured white bread (such as Pepperidge Farm)

3 slices smoked ham, ¼ inch thick, sliced in half lengthwise

HOLLANDAISE SAUCE

½ pound butter

3 egg yolks, at room temperature

1 tablespoon water

2 teaspoons Dijon mustard

large pinch cayenne

salt and freshly ground pepper

6 tablespoons melted butter

Lightly flatten chicken breasts. Melt butter in a large baking dish; add chicken in a single layer. Sprinkle with 1–2 tablespoons lemon juice, tarragon, salt and pepper; cover with waxed paper. Bake in a preheated 400 degree oven until springy to the touch, around 8 minutes; remove and keep warm.

While the chicken is baking, make the hollandaise sauce. Melt the butter, but do not boil; set aside. Place the egg yolks, water, mustard and remaining lemon juice in a blender or food processor. Add the warm butter beating slowly until thick. Season with cayenne, salt and pepper to taste; keep warm in a saucepan over hot water. Heat the ham and keep warm.

Cut the bread in half into triangles; brush with melted butter and toast lightly on each side; keep warm. In a large sauté pan bring salt water to a boil; add asparagus and blanch until tender crisp, about 2–3 minutes depending on thickness; drain and keep warm.

For each serving arrange 3 triangles of toast on a warm plate; top with ½ slice of ham, 5 spears of asparagus, chicken and dress with hollandaise sauce.

Serves 6

CREAM OF ASPARAGUS SOUP

A lovely cream soup that can be made a day early and enjoyed for a spring lunch or dinner.

1½ cups chopped, fresh asparagus without tips (save for garnish)

2½ cups chicken stock

4 tablespoons butter

½ cup chopped onions

5 tablespoons flour

½ cup dry white wine

1 cup heavy cream

¼ teaspoon dried basil

¼ teaspoon dried tarragon

salt, freshly ground pepper and nutmeg to taste

In a saucepan, boil the chopped asparagus in the chicken stock until almost tender. Strain the stock and set aside the cooked asparagus. In another saucepan, melt the butter and sauté the chopped onion until translucent, stirring often. Add flour, a little at a time, cook 2 or 3 minutes. To this mixture, add the reserved cooked asparagus; sauté 2 or 3 minutes stirring often. Add the stock, wine, cream, basil and tarragon and season with the salt, pepper and nutmeg. Cook 15–20 minutes until the asparagus is tender; cool slightly and blend in a blender until smooth. Add asparagus tips 30 minutes before serving and cook over low heat until tips are almost tender.

Serves 4–5

From robust hunter's stews
to country cheesecake

A TASTE OF POLAND

There is a phrase common to the Slavic people: "When a guest comes to the house, God comes with him." It is a phrase that well defines the Poles' mealtime hospitality and the full-flavored, satisfying meals they prepare.

No Polish dish is prepared with more care than their rich variety of soups. Most popular are beet *barszca klarowny,* duck *czarnina,* mushroom *zupa grzybowa,* and cabbage *kapusniak ze swiezej kapusty.* Most famous of all their hearty soups or stews is Hunter's Stew *bigos* made with Polish sausage and sauerkraut, and sometimes enriched with homemade noodles or small, filled noodles, similar to the Italian tortellini *uszka.*

Noodles made by Polish cooks are legendary. Pierogi is a favorite, and similar to the Italians' ravioli. The four-inch circles are cut from yeast or delicate noodle-pasta dough and filled with sweet or savory fillings of beef, cabbage, mushrooms, sauerkraut, potato, cheese or cooked fruit.

The pierogis are then simmered in broth, soup or water; sautéed in butter; or baked. They are served in soups, or as an appetizer, a side dish, an entree or a dessert.

Dumplings play a major role in Polish cuisine. Made of mashed potatoes, the delicate dumplings are stuffed with meat, sauerkraut, or cheese, and served with meats or poultry in place of potatoes.

Poles prepare mushrooms, wild, dried and domestic, in countless ways: lightly sautéed in butter, stuffed, puréed, marinated in vinegar and oil, mixed with sour cream, in puddings, shaped into patties or cutlets and fried, or simmered in rich soups.

Root vegetables are popular, including potatoes, beets, turnips, rutabagas, kohlrabi, cabbage, chard and cauliflower. Often cooked simply, they are served with a mushroom or sour cream sauce, or with buttered bread crumbs. Caraway, paprika and dill are frequent seasoners.

Polish desserts are rich and wonderful. There are chocolate and nut tortes, kolachys (jam-filled cookies), mazurkas (a shortbread-type pastry square with varying toppings), babkas (a rich yeast cake), and cheesecakes, most often made with cottage cheese.

Two favorites in Polish cuisine—
stuffed cabbage rolls with sour
cream and crescent-shaped
pierogi.

MUSHROOM SOUP
(Zupa Grzybowa)

A light first course that can become hearty fare with the addition of tiny Polish filled dumplings.

3 tablespoons butter

1 onion, chopped

8 ounces fresh mushrooms, sliced

2 tablespoons flour

4 cups vegetable or beef stock

½ teaspoon dried dill or 1½ tablespoons fresh dill, minced

4 tablespoons sour cream

salt and pepper

Melt butter in a stockpot, and sauté onion until lightly browned. Add mushrooms, and cook 3–4 minutes. Add flour, and cook over low flame about 5 minutes, stirring frequently. Add stock slowly, and blend until smooth. Simmer 10 minutes. Add dill, and stir in the sour cream. Heat through, and adjust seasonings.

Serves 4

POTATO PANCAKES
(Placki Z Kartofli)

Make extra pancakes, everyone will certainly want seconds and for a special touch, serve with homemade applesauce.

4 cups grated raw potatoes

4 tablespoons flour

3 well-beaten eggs

4 tablespoons finely chopped or grated onion

2 teaspoons salt and freshly ground black pepper to taste

2 teaspoons sugar

cooking oil and butter

Rinse grated potatoes in water; drain and press out excess water thoroughly. In large bowl, add all ingredients, and beat well. Heat large, heavy skillet, and add butter and equal amounts of salad oil to measure almost ¼ inch of fat in skillet. With spoon, drop pancake batter by heaping spoonfuls into skillet, and flatten batter with back of spoon as thinly as possible. Fry on both sides until crisp and brown. Serve very hot with sour cream and applesauce.

Serves 4

STUFFED CABBAGE ROLLS
(Golabki)

This slightly sweet entree is a unique variation on the traditional cabbage roll.

3 pound head of white cabbage

¼ cup long-grain rice

12 tablespoons butter

3 cups chopped onions

¾–1 pound lean ground beef

1 teaspoon salt

freshly ground black pepper

1 tablespoon fresh dill or 1 teaspoon dried dill weed

12–16 pitted prunes, soaked in cold water (15 minutes), and drained

2 tablespoons oil

3 medium tomatoes, peeled, seeded, and chopped

salt and pepper

1 tablespoon flour

½ cup sour cream

¼ cup fresh dill or 2 tablespoons dried dill weed

Cook cabbage in boiling water for 10 minutes. Remove outer leaves as they are cooked. Continue cooking until all leaves have been removed and cooked. Discard small inner leaves. Bring 2 cups water to boil and add rice; boil briskly, uncovered, for 12 minutes. Drain and set aside.

Melt 4 tablespoons butter in large skillet over high heat and add 2 cups onions. Stir occasionally and cook 8–10 minutes or until soft. Transfer to large bowl and add beef, cooked rice, 1 teaspoon salt, a few grindings from pepper mill and dill. Mix together. Lay cabbage leaves out and trim tough rib end from base of each leaf. Place ¼ cup of filling and 1 prune in center. Fold in edges and roll up tightly. Melt 4 tablespoons butter in skillet with oil. When foam subsides, add a few cabbage rolls, seam-side down and fry 3–5 minutes until golden. Do not burn.

Remove with slotted spoon to baking dish; do not stack. Repeat until filling is gone. Melt remaining butter and sauté last cup of chopped onions until soft. Stir in tomatoes, salt and pepper. In small mixing bowl, beat flour into sour cream one teaspoon at a time and stir mixture into simmering sauce. Adjust seasonings, and pour sauce over cabbage rolls, masking them completely. Bake uncovered in center of oven for 45 minutes at 350 degrees or until rolls are golden brown. Sprinkle with dill.

Serves 6

HUNTER'S STEW
(Bigos)

More meat may be used in this stew, and others such as lamb, ham, veal, venison, or rabbit may be added or substituted.

2 ounces salt pork, diced, or 4 slices thick bacon, diced

2 medium onions, sliced

1 leek, thinly sliced

1 pound fresh mushrooms, halved

10 tablespoons flour

1 tablespoon paprika

1 pound each beef and pork, cubed

cooking oil

2 cups beef stock

12 ounces kielbasa sausage, sliced

½ cup Madeira wine (sherry can be substituted)

1 pound sauerkraut, rinsed and drained

small boiled potatoes

2 tablespoons parsley, minced

salt and pepper

Fry pork or bacon until golden, but not crisp, in large Dutch oven. Add onions and leeks. Sauté 3 minutes on low heat. Add mushrooms, sauté 3–4 minutes. Add 2 tablespoons flour, and cook 1–2 minutes. Remove ingredients from pan.

Combine remaining flour and paprika, and dredge beef and pork cubes. Add oil to pan. Brown meat, adding oil as needed. Return vegetables to Dutch oven, and add stock, kielbasa, wine, and sauerkraut to pan. Mix and bring to a boil, reduce heat, cover and simmer 1½–2 hours or until meat is tender. Add boiled potatoes and parsley and cook 5 minutes or until heated through. Taste and adjust seasonings and serve in large bowls with slices of rye bread.

Serves 6

PIEROGI

These wonderful dumplings have either a vegetable or sweetened cheese filling. Serve boiled or fried for appetizers or in soup at dinner or lunch.

2 cups flour
1 teaspoon salt
3 tablespoons butter, cut into small pieces
1 egg
water
cheese or cabbage and mushroom filling

In large bowl with pastry blender or in food processor, blend flour and salt well, and add butter until well incorporated. In measuring cup, combine egg and enough water to total ⅔ cup of liquid; add this mixture in small amounts to dry ingredients, making a stiff but pliable dough. Do not handle dough too much; wrap in waxed paper or plastic wrap and let sit for 30 minutes. Roll dough thinly, and cut with three-inch biscuit cutter. Fill with about 1 tablespoon filling, and fold in half, making sure filling does not get on edges; pinch edges together, making a good seal. Place pierogis in boiling water—only a few at one time. When they rise to water surface, remove them. Repeat until all are cooked. Pierogis may be served either boiled with butter and sour cream, fried in butter until golden brown on both sides, or placed in a buttered, covered casserole with ½ cup sour cream and heated in oven. However you prepare them, serve with sour cream.

Makes 18–20 3-inch pierogis

CHEESE FILLING
(Z Serem)
makes 2½ cups

1¼ pounds or 2½ cups bakers cheese, soft farmer cheese or a combination of dry-curd cottage cheese and ricotta cheese, well blended.
3 tablespoons sugar
1 egg, beaten
½ teaspoon salt
¼ teaspoon grated lemon rind

In a bowl, mix all the above ingredients until well combined.

CABBAGE AND MUSHROOM FILLING
(Kapusta Z Grzybami)
makes 3 cups

1 small head of cabbage
1 small onion, chopped fine
2 tablespoons butter
2 cups chopped mushrooms
2 tablespoons sour cream
salt and pepper

Quarter and chop cabbage finely, and cook in salted water for 10 minutes; drain and set aside. Sauté onion in butter 2 minutes; add mushrooms, and continue to sauté 5 minutes; add cabbage, and continue to cook 30–45 minutes until flavors have blended. Add sour cream, and mix well. Add salt and pepper to taste.

Serves 8

ROAST LOIN OF PORK
(Schab Pieczony)

The usual pork richness is subdued in this dish with the addition of a spicy applesauce topping. Serve it with cheese or potato pierogis and a fruit compote.

2 tablespoons flour
1½ teaspoons salt
1 teaspoon dry mustard
½ teaspoon caraway seed
½ teaspoon sugar
¼ teaspoon freshly ground black pepper
¼ teaspoon dried sage
1 boneless pork roast (4–5 pounds), tied

TOPPING
1½ cups applesauce
½ cup brown sugar
¼ teaspoon cinnamon or allspice
¼ teaspoon mace
¼ teaspoon salt

Mix flour, salt, mustard, caraway seed, sugar, pepper and sage. Untie roast, rub mixture over entire surface and retie roast. Set in roasting pan and roast at 325 degrees for 1½ hours.

Mix applesauce with brown sugar, cinnamon or allspice, mace and salt. Spread on top of meat. Roast about 45 minutes longer or until done. Remove from oven, and allow to sit 5 minutes before slicing.

Serves 8

COUNTRY CHEESECAKE

This old world dessert is not as rich as most cheesecakes, it just tastes that way. Like all cheesecakes, make it at least one or two days ahead—they improve in flavor and slicing is much easier.

PASTRY
6 tablespoons butter, softened
1 cup flour
½ teaspoon salt
2 tablespoons sugar
1 egg yolk
1 tablespoon milk

FILLING
1 pound cottage cheese
1 cup sugar
¼ cup flour
¼ teaspoon salt
4 egg yolks
½ cup heavy cream
2 ounces rum or 1 teaspoon rum extract
½ cup candied orange peel, finely chopped
5 egg whites

To make pastry, combine butter with flour, salt and sugar and toss until well blended. Add egg yolk and milk and mix well. Form into ball, cover and chill 1 hour. Roll or press into bottom of 9- or 10-inch springform pan. Prebake at 400 degrees for 5 minutes. Cool a few minutes on wire rack. Turn oven down to 350 degrees.

To make filling, blend cottage cheese until smooth in food processor or blender. Transfer to bowl and combine with sugar, flour and salt. Beat egg yolks and add to cheese mixture. Add cream, rum and orange peel. Beat egg whites until stiff. Fold into cheese mixture carefully. Pour over prebaked shell and return to oven. Bake 50–60 minutes or until knife inserted in center comes out clean. Cool on wire rack. Cake will settle slightly. Serve when completely cool.

Serves 8

EASTER BRUNCH

If you're looking for a variation of your traditional Easter dinner, you might consider forgetting dinner altogether, and entertain your family and friends with a full course Easter brunch. Center it around eggs—what could be more in the Easter tradition!

In some cultures it was protocol to present the hostess of the Easter festivities with a handsomely decorated Easter egg, one made of porcelain, paper, glass, jewels; or edible ones of chocolate or marzipan. While eating cooked eggs was once forbidden during Lent, they were lavishly decorated for later consumption. Symbolizing continuing life, they were often painted bright red, and were thought to bring good luck and help keep one's house free from evil. On Easter morning, they were the first food eaten.

Eggs can be served in a variety of delectable and satisfying dishes—soufflés, quiches, omelets, casseroles—either as main courses or accompaniments to ham, sausage or fish. Depending on your heritage or just simply your culinary taste, choose a traditional Easter bread to complement your menu.

The Greeks are known for their *tsoureki,* a cross-shaped yeast bread, adorned with a cluster of red eggs; Italians make a spicy bread using the same technique. Eastern Europeans bake *kulich* with nuts and raisins and serve it with *pashka,* a rich cheese, cream and butter spread. The Polish make *babka wielkanocna* or Easter baba, a leavened cake. And Finns serve *paasiaisleipa,* a mushroom-shaped yeast bread with cardamon and candied fruit. Other traditions include hot cross buns, biscuits, muffins, popovers, waffles, pancakes and French toast.

Serve a variety of beverages, hot and cold, with and without alochol. Mineral water with a twist of lemon or lime and iced teas are easily prepared. With a little more preparation, serve up frothy hot chocolate with a hint of amaretto, crème de cacao or crème de menthe; strong-flavored coffees; or even champagne.

Easter brunch with parsley-chive biscuits, ham with ginger-brandy sauce and eggs in nests with Mornay sauce.

EASTER BRUNCH CITRUS SALAD

On the night before your brunch, peel and section the oranges and grapefruit, wash the greens and make the dressing.

4 oranges, peeled, sectioned and sliced in half

2 grapefruits, peeled, sectioned, and sliced in thirds

1 large head of romaine lettuce, exclude outer leaves

1 bunch watercress

2 tablespoons grated Swiss or Gruyère cheese

1 cup alfalfa sprouts

½ cup green pepper, cut in thin slivers

DRESSING

½ cup vegetable oil

4 tablespoons fresh lemon juice

2 tablespoons honey

1 tablespoon chopped fresh chives

¼ teaspoon salt

⅛ teaspoon coarsely grated black pepper

Wash greens. Tear romaine in large bite-sized pieces and remove large stems from watercress. On large platter, arrange romaine, watercress and orange and grapefruit sections. Sprinkle with green pepper and grated cheese. Decorate with sprouts. Cover and refrigerate.

Place all dressing ingredients in jar with tight fitting lid; cover and shake. Just before serving, pour dressing over the salad and toss.

Salad recipe can be prepared to this point up to 4 hours in advance.

Serves 10–12

SPINACH AND CHEESE TART

A brunch dish that couldn't be simpler. Make and partially bake the pastry a day ahead, as well as the filling. Early the next day, just assemble and bake.

1 recipe of pâte brisée or 10-inch piecrust

1 pound ricotta cheese

3 tablespoons sour cream

6 tablespoons freshly grated Parmesan cheese

2 tablespoons flour

2 eggs

1½ teaspoons dried basil

1 tablespoon fresh parsley, chopped

2 tablespoons green onions, chopped and sautéed in 1 tablespoon butter for 2 minutes

½ teaspoon grated lemon rind

freshly grated nutmeg

salt and freshly ground pepper

10 ounces fresh spinach, washed, cooked until just wilted, chopped and squeezed well, or 1-10 ounce package frozen chopped spinach, cooked and squeezed of all its liquid

¼ pound cooked ham, cut into julienned slivers

Preheat oven to 350 degrees. Bake pastry shell for 10–15 minutes; set aside to cool.

Place ricotta cheese, 4 tablespoons Parmesan cheese, sour cream, flour, and eggs in large bowl. Beat at high speed with electric mixer until mixture is smooth; add salt and pepper.

Mix half of cheese mixture with spinach and add basil, parsley, sautéed green onions, lemon rind and nutmeg.

Spread the spinach and cheese mixture on bottom of partially baked pastry shell. Lay julienned ham slices on top of spinach; press down lightly. Carefully spread plain cheese mixture on top of spinach and ham. Sprinkle remaining 2 tablespoons Parmesan cheese on top. Bake 40 minutes. Serve immediately.

PÂTE BRISÉE

1¼ cups flour

6 tablepoons cold butter cut into bits

2 tablespoons vegetable shortening

¼ teaspoon salt

3 tablespoons ice water

In large bowl with pastry blender (or in food processor), blend flour, butter, vegetable shortening and salt until mixture resembles meal. Slowly add ice water, toss mixture until water is just incorporated and form dough into ball. Knead dough lightly with heel of hand against smooth, cool surface for a few seconds to distribute shortening and form into flat circle. Dust dough with flour; cover and chill for 1 hour. Roll out dough and fit into 10-inch tart pan with removable bottom.

Serves 10–12

BAKED HAM WITH GINGER-BRANDY SAUCE

A succulent, easy-to-make ham with the unique combination of orange, brandy, currant, honey, mustard and ginger.

1 fully cooked semi-boneless smoked ham (about 6 pounds)

whole cloves

grated zest (peel) of 1 orange

½ cup fresh orange juice

½ cup brandy

3 tablespoons currant jelly

⅓ cup honey

2 tablespoons dry mustard

1 teaspoon ground ginger

Preheat oven to 300 degrees. Remove rind from ham; score fat on top of ham in diamond pattern; insert cloves in center of each diamond. Sprinkle ham with orange zest and pour orange juice into pan. Bake in center of oven for 45 minutes, basting frequently. Combine brandy, currant jelly, honey, dry mustard and ginger in blender. Blend at low speed until mixture is smooth. Spoon glaze over ham and continue baking until ham is deep brown, basting frequently, about 45 minutes. Let ham stand 10 minutes before carving. Serve with assorted mustards.

Serves 10–12

EGGS IN NESTS

The Mornay sauce and mushrooms filling can be made in advance—a boon for the busy hostess.

1 pound thin egg noodles

10–12 eggs

MORNAY SAUCE

5 tablepoons butter

6 tablespoons flour

4½ cups milk

½ cup Parmesan cheese

¾ cup grated Swiss cheese

1 teaspoon dried tarragon

2 tablespoons minced onion

3 tablespoons white wine

dash of Tabasco

1 teaspoon salt

¼ teaspoon white pepper

3 tablespoons fresh parsley, chopped

MUSHROOM FILLING:

1 pound fresh mushrooms, thinly sliced

4 tablespoons butter

4 tablespoons fresh lemon juice

⅓ cup sliced green onions

½ teaspoon Dijon mustard

salt and pepper to taste

Prepare Mornay sauce: In a saucepan melt butter; add flour and minced onions, and cook for 2–3 minutes whisking constantly. Slowly add milk; continue to whisk until thick. Add Parmesan and Swiss cheeses; continue to cook until cheeses are melted. Add tarragon, wine, Tabasco, salt, and pepper and parsley. Adjust seasonings and set aside.

Prepare mushroom filling: In sauté pan melt butter. Sprinkle lemon juice over mushrooms and toss. Add mushrooms, green onions and mustard to melted butter in pan and cook until juices are cooked down. Add salt and pepper to taste. Set aside.

Cook noodles according to package directions, drain. Place noodles in large pan and add half Mornay sauce. Mix well.

Preheat oven to 325 degrees. Butter large ovenproof dish and form little nests, each with ⅔ cup of noodles, with center indentations. Make 10–12 nests. In bottom of each nest, add about 2 tablespoons of mushroom filling; press with spoon to maintain the nest indentation. Break eggs carefully, place one raw egg in each indentation and add salt and pepper. Cover dish tightly, and bake about 20 minutes depending on how hard you wish the yolk to be. With knife cut around each nest for easier serving. Nap the nests with remaining warm Mornay sauce.

Serves 10–12

PARSLEY-CHIVE BISCUITS

These biscuits are best when served fresh and hot from the oven.

3 cups flour

2½ tablespoons sugar

4½ teaspoons baking powder

¾ teaspoon baking soda

¾ teaspoon salt

1 stick (8 tablespoons) butter, cut into bits

¼ cup lard

½ cup buttermilk

½ cup fresh minced parsley

3 tablespoons fresh minced chives

1 egg, lightly beaten

Sift together flour, sugar, baking powder, baking soda and salt in large bowl. Blend in butter and lard until mixture resembles meal. With fork stir in parsley, chives and ¼ cup of buttermilk (or enough to bind dough) and egg. Turn dough out onto floured surface, knead once or twice and pat into ¾-inch-thick round. Cut dough with decorative cookie cutters (pigs, bunnies, lambs, etc.) or a biscuit cutter. Bake on buttered baking sheet in preheated 400 degree oven for 15 minutes or until golden.

16 biscuits

APRICOT POUND CAKE

The apricot, brandy and rum transforms this cake from the traditional pound cake into holiday splendor.

2 sticks (1 cup) unsalted butter, softened

3 cups sugar

6 large eggs

1 cup sour cream

½ cup plus 1 tablespoon apricot brandy

1 teaspoon vanilla

1 teaspoon orange extract

1 teaspoon rum extract or 1 tablespoon dark rum

½ cup dried apricots, chopped

grated zest (peel) of 1 orange

3 cups sifted all-purpose flour

½ teaspoon salt

¼ teaspoon baking soda

In small bowl, soak chopped apricots in 4 tablespoons of apricot brandy. Set aside for 15 minutes.

In large bowl, cream butter, add sugar a little at a time, beating well, until light and fluffy. Add eggs, one at a time, beating well after each addition. Beat in sour cream, soaked apricots, remaining apricot brandy, vanilla, orange extract, rum extract and orange zest. In bowl sift together flour, salt and baking soda. Stir dry mixture into butter mixture. Transfer batter into well-buttered and floured 2½-quart bundt pan and bake cake in preheated slow oven (325 degrees) for 1 hour and 15 minutes, or until the cake tests done. Let cake cool in pan on rack for 45 minutes; invert on plate and brush on Apricot Glaze.

APRICOT GLAZE

1 cup fresh orange juice

⅔ cup sugar

½ cup dried apricots, chopped very fine

3 tablespoons apricot brandy

In small saucepan, add orange juice, sugar and apricots. Cook over low heat until sugar liquefies. Bring to low boil, remove from heat and add apricot brandy. While glaze is still warm, apply to cake.

Serves 14–15

SALUTING SPINACH

Putting aside childhood memories of dinner plates filled with hot green stuff that never seemed to disappear, spinach deserves a little respect. More than likely the stuff many of us detested was over-cooked, becoming stringy and bitter in the process. But treat spinach right and you'll appreciate it as a full-flavored, healthful and versatile vegetable.

For the home gardener, there are several varieties suitable for the Wisconsin climate. Bloomsdale is the choice for early planting. It grows best in cool, moist weather of spring and fall. The leaves are thick-textured, dark green and crinkled —the type most frequently found in grocery stores. Bloomsdale is best when picked young, and is delicious raw as well as cooked. Once the weather turns hot, this variety goes to seed and becomes tough and inedible.

The New Zealand variety, on the other hand, withstands heat and is slow to bolt, and summer planting is actually preferable. Raw, it has a rather bland taste, but cooked it is one of the most flavorful.

Good spinach is brightly colored and crisp, with either long, flat pointed leaves or thick and curly ones. If you purchase it packaged, discard any yellowed, wilted or mushy leaves before refrigerating, then store, unwashed, in a plastic bag with holes for circulation. Spinach has a high water content and is very perishable.

Because the leaves are a trap for soil and sand, thorough washing is essential.

Fill a kitchen basin with lukewarm water, swish the leaves around, drain, and repeat this process until no residue of soil or sand remains in the basin.

To remove the stems from the larger leaves, fold each leaf in half lengthwise, so that the vein faces you, and starting at the stem end, rip down. When spinach is to be used raw, drain and dry the leaves on paper towels or in a salad spinner.

The easiest cooking method, which also retains maximum nutrients, is to place the washed leaves in a skillet; the little water clinging to them is enough for cooking. Cover the skillet and place it over medium heat for three to four minutes, until the spinach leaves are wilted but remain bright green. (Avoid using aluminum pans; the spinach reacts to the metal and turns grey, picking up an acid taste.) Remove the spinach, and drain and squeeze it completely dry in paper towels. Season it with salt and pepper, freshly ground nutmeg and butter; with croutons, toasted almonds or pine nuts; or with a little cream, grated Swiss or Parmesan cheese.

The great taste of spinach in Turban of sole with spinach and salmon mousses, and tart Sauce Veloute with capers.

SPINACH SALAD

Make the dressing the night before allowing the flavors to mellow. Place dressing on salad just before serving and toss lightly.

1 pound fresh spinach, washed and stemmed

2 cans water chestnuts, rinsed and thinly sliced

1½ cups bean sprouts or fresh mushrooms, thinly sliced

2 hard boiled eggs, chopped coarsely

8 strips of bacon fried until crisp, drained and chopped

DRESSING
1 cup vegetable oil

½ cup sugar

⅓ cup ketchup

¼ cup cider vinegar

1 tablespoon Worcestershire sauce

1 medium onion minced

½ teaspoon salt

⅛ cayenne pepper

In a jar with a lid combine all the dressing ingredients, shake and let stand overnight. In a large salad bowl or on individual salad dishes, tear the large spinach leaves, add the water chestnuts, sprouts or mushrooms, egg and bacon. Toss with the dressing and sprinkle with freshly ground black pepper.

Serves 8

TURBAN OF SOLE

This beautiful entree takes some time to prepare, but once the praises start coming in, all your efforts will be worth it. One stepsaver is to prepare the mousses early in the day and keep them refrigerated.

1¼–1½ pounds thin sole fillets

SAUCE FOR SPINACH AND SALMON MOUSSES
3 tablespoons butter

2 tablespoons minced shallots

5 tablespoons flour

1 cup milk, room temperature

4 egg yolks, lightly beaten

2 tablespoons dry vermouth or white wine

salt and freshly ground pepper

In saucepan, melt butter, add shallots and saute until soft. Whisk in flour, stirring well and remove from heat. Gradually add milk and whisk until smooth. Cook over low heat, stirring constantly until thick. Remove from heat and carefully beat in egg yolks, adding only small amounts at a time and incorporating well. Whisk in vermouth, and heat 1 minute. Season and set aside.

BASE FOR SPINACH AND SALMON MOUSSE
4 egg whites

pinch of salt

pinch of cream of tartar

Beat egg whites with cream of tartar and salt until stiff, and set aside.

SPINACH MOUSSE
2 tablespoons butter

3 tablespoons green onions, minced

12 ounces fresh spinach, cleaned, stemmed, steamed, rinsed in cold water, squeezed dry and chopped

½ teaspoon freshly grated nutmeg

salt and freshly ground pepper

In skillet, melt butter, add the onions and sauté until soft. Add spinach to onions, and sauté 1 minute. Remove to large bowl, add nutmeg and half of sauce for mousses and combine well. Fold ½ of egg-white base into spinach mixture. Season to taste and set aside.

SALMON MOUSSE
1 pound fresh salmon, filleted

2 tablespoons fresh dill

1 teaspoon dried tarragon

1 tablespoon fresh lemon juice

grated lemon peel

cayenne pepper

salt and freshly ground pepper

In food processor, grind salmon, then mix in remaining sauce for mousses, dill, tarragon, lemon juice and peel and cayenne. Remove to large bowl and fold in remaining egg-white base. Season to taste and set aside.

Assembly
Pat dry sole fillets. In well-buttered 2-quart, 9″×12″ ring mold (preferably Pyrex or ceramic), arrange fillets, slightly overlapping with some hanging over edge. Spread spinach mousse evenly over fillets and top with salmon mousse. Fold fish fillets over salmon mousse, and cover with buttered wax paper (can be refrigerated at this point if covered with plastic wrap up to 4 hours).

To cook, place in a pan of hot water, deep enough to cover half of mold and bake 30–35 minutes at 350 degrees. Pour off excess liquid and after 5 minutes turn onto platter. Blot excess liquid, and serve hot with Sauce Veloute.

SAUCE VELOUTE WITH CAPERS
1 cup fish stock or clam juice

1 cup dry white wine

3 tablespoons butter

3–4 tablespoons flour

2 tablespoons minced shallots

¼–½ cup heavy cream

4 tablespoons butter

2 tablespoons capers

2 tablespoons lemon juice or add to taste

salt and freshly ground pepper

In large saucepan, rapidly boil down fish stock and wine to little over half of original amount. In another saucepan, make roux with butter, flour and shallots. Whisk until they foam and froth for about 2 minutes (do not brown). Whisk in hot cooking juices and blend until smooth, bringing to boil. Boil 2 minutes, adding additional stock if needed. Slowly add cream and whisk. Add additional butter slowly, blending well. Add capers and lemon juice. Adjust seasoning, and serve with the turban.

Serves 8

SPINACH AND BACON STUFFED CHICKEN BREASTS

This piquant, hot sauce is reminiscent of the old favorite hot bacon dressing served on spinach salads.

4 whole chicken breasts, skinned, boned and halved

8 strips bacon

4 scallions, minced

1 clove garlic, minced

1 pound fresh spinach, blanched, squeezed dry and chopped

1 egg, lightly beaten

½ cup croutons, lightly crushed

¼ teaspoon thyme

¼ teaspoon marjoram

salt and pepper

butter and oil

flour

Sauce (recipe follows)

Cook the 8 strips of bacon until crisp. Remove, drain and crumble; set aside. Discard all but 2 tablespoons drippings. Sauté the scallions and garlic in drippings and remove from heat. Add spinach, egg, croutons, thyme, marjoram, salt, pepper and reserved bacon. Mix well. Taste and adjust seasonings.

Flatten chicken breasts between wax paper and pound with a mallet or rolling pin. Spread an equal portion of the spinach-bacon filling to within ½ inch of the edge. Tuck in ends and roll. Secure with sturdy toothpicks. Sprinkle with flour. In another skillet, add an equal amount of oil and butter. Place in chicken rolls and sauté 8–10 minutes, cover part of the time. When done, remove and keep warm.

SAUCE

8 slices bacon

4 scallions, minced

1 tablespoon sugar

4 tablespoons vinegar

1 tablespoon cornstarch mixed with ½ cup chicken stock

salt and freshly ground pepper

¼ teaspoon thyme

¼ teaspoon marjoram

Cook bacon until crisp. Remove, drain and crumble; set aside. In 3 tablespoons of drippings, sauté the scallions. Add the sugar, vinegar, thyme and marjoram and cook 1 minute. Add the cornstarch-stock mixture slowly. Cook until smooth. Adjust seasonings. Serve immediately over chicken rolls.

Serves 8

SPINACH SOUP

A light, delicate, colorful soup to be served as a first course with a chicken, veal or lamb entree.

1 small onion, finely chopped

1 leek, halved and thinly sliced

1 large garlic clove, minced

4 tablespoons butter

2 cups raw potato, peeled and diced

3 cups beef stock

1 pound fresh spinach, cleaned and stemmed

1 cup cream

1 cup diced ham

⅛ teaspoon freshly ground nutmeg

salt

⅛ teaspoon freshly ground pepper

Parmesan cheese

In large saucepan, sauté onion, leek, and garlic in butter for 3–4 minutes, until soft. Add potato, stock and spinach and simmer for 15–20 minutes, until potatoes are done.

Purée half soup mixture; return to saucepan. Add cream, ham, nutmeg, and salt and pepper to taste. Heat to boiling. Serve with 1 tablespoon Parmesan cheese in each bowl.

Serves 8

SPINACH PASTRY TRIANGLES

These appetizers can be frozen ahead of time and baked just before serving—no need to thaw.

SPINACH AND CHEESE FILLING

3 tablespoons butter

2 tablespoons olive oil

½ cup scallions, chopped

1 pound spinach, cleaned, stemmed, steamed, squeezed dry, and chopped

¼ pound feta cheese, drained and crumbled

¼ pound ricotta cheese

½ cup fresh parsley, chopped

¼ cup fresh dill, chopped

2 eggs, slightly beaten

1 teaspoon grated lemon peel

salt and freshly ground pepper

In skillet, melt butter and add oil. Sauté scallions until soft; add spinach and combine well. Continue to sauté for 1 or 2 minutes. Remove to large bowl, and add the cheeses, parsley, dill, eggs and lemon. Mix well and adjust seasoning. Set aside.

PHYLLO TRIANGLES

1 pound package phyllo, thawed

½ pound butter

In small saucepan, melt butter and set aside. Lay one sheet of phyllo on flat work surface. Brush lightly with butter; cover with second sheet of phyllo and continue with third. Cut sheets in half lengthwise; then cut each half crosswise into 6 equal parts or 4 for larger triangles. Spoon one teaspoon (or two teaspoons for larger triangles) of filling onto the end of each strip, and fold up forming a triangle using a classic flag-folding technique. Continue process until all of filling is used. Place on buttered baking sheet; brush with butter, and bake in preheated 400 degree oven for about 10 minutes until golden.

Approximately 50 triangles

Lamb, leeks and potatoes with an herbal flair

SPRING MENU

When it's time to bring the freshness of a Wisconsin spring to the table, there are some wonderfully good choices to make. It is the season for tender, young lamb (no more than twenty months old), new potatoes, asparagus and leeks, all cooked in savory spring-fresh herbs.

Fresh lamb meat should be treated like any quality red meat—avoid high temperatures and overcooking. One of the most simple and succulent preparations is roasted leg of lamb. Roast it on the bone in the oven or on a barbeque grill, or cook it butterflied (boneless), smothered with garlic, rosemary or mint. Insert a thermometer in the thickest part of the leg (but not touching a bone) and roast for twelve to fifteen minutes per pound at 125 to 130 degrees for rare meat or twenty minutes per pound at 140 degrees for medium. It is most tender when still slightly pink on the inside. The meat should be basted frequently after the initial first hour of roasting.

There are equally tasty dishes that utilize cheaper cuts. The shoulder, for example, is extremely flavorful. Since it is less tender, this cut should be marinated and used in shish kebabs or braised in cubes for pilafs. In preparing any cut of lamb, trim off the excess fat and remove the thin membrane layer. If the meat has been marinating, remove it from the marinade half an hour before cooking. Bringing the meat to room temperature first allows some of the marinade to evaporate, which perks up the flavor of the meat.

Because lamb tastes best when it's hot, warm all platters and individual dishes just before serving.

Tender green peas, young and flavorful new red potatoes, fresh leeks and asparagus are all excellent accompaniments to a lamb dish. While taste for these vegetables vary, new potatoes—the small, red, waxy varieties—seem to be everyone's favorites. It is their high moisture content that gives them a waxy consistency, and they are best when boiled or steamed.

While the most common use for leeks is to flavor stews or soups, like vichyssoise, it is delicious in combination with other vegetables. Available most of the year, it is particularly tasty in the small, young varieties of spring. Oversized bulbs usually indicate second year crops and are rather fibrous. Leeks should have vivid green, wilt-free tops, and the white portion should be relatively long and free of soft spots and blemishes. Store leeks in plastic bags in the refrigerator, washing and trimming them just before using. A leek tart or julienned leeks and vegetables in mustard butter will add the perfect zest to a lamb dinner.

Serve the best of spring with roast leg of lamb in herb sauce, julienned vegetables and new potatoes.

SPRING SALAD

This salad makes use of the freshest of spring produce and can be varied depending on availability of ingredients and your taste.

1 cup mushrooms, sliced

6 radishes, sliced

1 cup peas, if fresh, blanched, if frozen, thawed

1½ cups asparagus, blanched and sliced lengthwise into 1-inch pieces

1½ tablespoons chives, chopped

1 head Boston, leaf or romaine lettuce, torn into large pieces

4 tablespoons red wine vinegar, or other flavored vinegar

2 tablespoons fresh lemon juice

2 tablespoons cream

2 teaspoons Dijon mustard

1 teaspoon salt

freshly ground pepper

1½ cups oil, vegetable or combination vegetable and olive oil

1 teaspoon sugar

2 tablespoons fresh chives

In a blender combine the vinegar, lemon juice, cream, mustard, salt and pepper. Slowly add the oil, sugar and chives. Adjust seasoning and set aside. In a large bowl combine the mushrooms, radishes, peas, asparagus and chives. Pour half of the dressing over the ingredients and set aside. Line 4 or 5 salad plates with lettuce. Divide mushroom-pea mixture over center of lettuce. Drizzle with some of the remaining dressing. Top with fresh ground pepper.

Serves 4–5

NEW POTATOES WITH SPRING HERBS

To save time, steam tiny new potatoes in a wok for just a few minutes, they should still have a bite, and refrigerate until just before sautéing.

2½–3 pounds new potatoes, with skins intact, steamed

2–3 tablespoons butter

1½–2 tablespoons finely minced mixed fresh herbs, (parsley, chives, tarragon, mint and / or chervil)

Melt butter in large skillet, add herbs and potatoes. Saute until just coated and heated through. Adjust seasonings and serve at once.

Serves 6

JULIENNED LEEKS AND VEGETABLES IN MUSTARD BUTTER

When cleaning leeks, remove withered outer leaves, cut off base and upper green leaves down to where the dark green begins to change color. Slice in half and rinse gently under running water.

2 leeks, cleaned, split, and julienned (matchstick width and about 4 in. long or ¼ × 4 inches)

¾ pounds thin asparagus, julienned

5 large carrots, julienned

¼ cup chicken stock

Place stock in skillet and bring to a boil; add largest and thickest vegetables first; cover carrots and cook 4 minutes. Add thick part of leeks. Cover and cook 2 minutes; add thinner carrots. Add bottom portion of asparagus; cover and cook 1 minute; add remaining asparagus; cook 1 minute longer. Remove and drain. Place on platter. Add mustard butter and toss. May be served warm or at room temperature.

MUSTARD BUTTER
½ stick butter

1 teaspoon herb or Dijon mustard

1 teaspoon dill weed, fresh

1 teaspoon minced chives

white pepper and salt

½ teaspoon lemon juice

Cream butter with mustard. Add lemon juice and mix well. Add dill and chives with dash of pepper and salt.

Serves 6

ROAST LAMB IN HERB SAUCE

A full-flavored lamb dish with a lovely sauce—do not overcook meat, maintain a nice pink color inside.

1 leg of lamb 6–7 pounds

4½ cups dry white wine

3 small onions, peeled and stuck with cloves

3 garlic cloves, crushed

12 peppercorns

14 juniper berries

salt

2 carrots, scraped and quartered

6 parsley sprigs

3 bay leaves

3 fresh mint sprigs, or 1½ teaspoon dried mint

1 teaspoon dried thyme

¼ cup salad oil

3 tablespoons finely chopped shallots or finely chopped scallions

3 tablespoons butter

1½ tablespoons flour

1½ cup flavored beef stock

¼ cup chopped parsley

2 tablespoons Madeira

Wipe leg of lamb with damp cloth. Place in stainless steel or ceramic or enamelware container. Mix wine with onions, garlic, peppercorns, juniper berries, 2 teaspoons salt, carrots, parsley, bay leaves, mint and thyme. Pour mixture over lamb. Let lamb marinate in refrigerator overnight. Preheat oven to hot (450 degrees). Remove lamb from marinade and dry well. Reserve marinade.

Place lamb on rack in roasting pan, rub with oil and sprinkle on additional salt and pepper. Roast lamb for 15 minutes, reduce oven heat to 350 degrees and continue to roast for 15 minutes to the pound —or longer if well done meat is desired. Baste frequently with juices.

Strain marinade and place in saucepan. Cook over high heat until reduced to almost half. Cook flour in butter whisking continuously about one minute; add shallots or scallions and continue to cook until they soften and start to turn golden. Add the reduced marinade slowly and then the flavored beef stock and Madeira; bring to a boil and then reduce heat, simmering 10 minutes. Add parsley and season with additional salt and pepper if necessary. Serve hot with lamb.

Serves 12

FRESH FRUIT TART

Use whatever fresh fruits are available; rings of sliced strawberries, kiwi, blueberries, raspberries, grape halves and even banana slices create a beautiful and tasty contrast to the Amaretto cream base and macaroon crust.

PASTRY

¾ cup cold butter, cut in tablespoon pieces

3 tablespoons powdered sugar

¼ teaspoon salt

1¼ cups flour

½ teaspoon anise extract

½ cup macaroon crumbs (dry)

FILLING

8 ounces cream cheese, softened

4 tablespoons sugar

2 teaspoons lemon rind, grated

2 teaspoons fresh lemon juice

2 teaspoons grated orange rind

5 tablespoons Amaretto

TOPPING

2 cups assorted fresh fruit, sliced

GLAZE

⅔ cup apricot preserves

2 tablespoons fresh lemon juice

In a food processor or bowl combine butter, sugar, salt, flour and anise extract. Whirl until it resembles meal. Stir in macaroon crumbs. Press into an 8″ removable bottom tart pan. Bake for 25 minutes in a preheated 350 degree oven or until golden brown. Cool.

In a food processor or bowl, combine the cream cheese and sugar until smooth. Add remaining filling ingredients, continue to process 4–5 seconds until well combined. Pour into baked crust, smooth and chill several hours.

Arrange cut fruit attractively on tart filling just before serving. Warm apricot preserves in a small saucepan, strain and stir in lemon juice. Brush glaze on top of fresh fruit and serve.

Serves 8–10

Recipes to make the dining
as good as the fishing

CATCH OF THE DAY

You've just had a great day on the water, caught a mess of panfish, a stringer of walleye, maybe a trophy salmon or muskie. Great feeling. Fishing's a challenging, satisfying sport. But all too often that's where the fun ends—how to *cook* those prize catches is often a mystery.

The first step in demystifying fish cookery is to acquaint yourself with the many species. Fish are categorized as either dry or oily, and preparation for each varies. Lean fish—pike, white fish, bass, lake perch—are the driest and mildest, and taste best when fried, sautéed, stuffed or baked in sauces. Oily fish—trout, catfish, salmon—have a slightly dark tint to the flesh and retain more moisture when cooked. These varieties generally benefit from baking, broiling or grilling; frying tends to make them greasy. Of course, there are exceptions—like small trout. Trout is the glamour fish: rich, moist and very flavorful and often the pride of restaurants with appealing entrees like *trout almondine, trout a la meuniere* and *trout au bleu*—a dish in which freshly caught trout is poached in aromatic vegetables and vinegar turning the flesh to a pleasant blue tinge.

Before any cleaning or cooking is done, be sure your fish is really fresh. If a friend gives it to you, ask how long ago it was caught; if purchased from a grocery store or seafood shop, ask the owner when it came in. You're safe if no more than two days have elapsed. In any case, the eyes should be bright, clear and protruding; the flesh should spring back when touched; and there should be no unpleasant odor.

Just before using, rinse under cold water and pat dry. If you're not going to prepare it that day, cover with plastic wrap and store no more than two days in your refrigerator. For longer storage, wrap in heavy paper or submerge in water and pack in airtight containers (wax milk cartons work well) and freeze.

When estimating portions, figure one-third pound of fillets per person or one pound of whole fish per person. The simplest way to cook small whole fish or fillets is by sautéeing or panfrying. Heat butter or bacon drippings in a skillet until hot but not smoking. Dust the fish with flour or cornmeal and fry until golden brown, turning only once. Remove to a platter and sprinkle with lemon juice, bacon pieces and minced parsley, or add approximately one-half cup heavy cream to the pan, cook it down slightly and pour over the fish.

Measuring the thickest part of the fish with a ruler, calculate the cooking time based on ten minutes per inch. This measurement is taken with the fish on its side, whether flat, rolled or stuffed and applies to any cooking method. If you bake it in a sauce, add five minutes more per inch of thickness, and twenty minutes more for each inch if frozen. Cooked fish should flake easily and the flesh should change from transparent to opaque.

A mustard-dill sauce spices up

Wisconsin beer batter fish.

HOMEMADE MAYONNAISE

Change the flavor of homemade mayonnaise by substituting different mustards, herb-accented vinegars and dried herbs —it will keep 3 to 4 weeks covered and refrigerated.

1 large whole egg or 3 egg yolks

1 teaspoon Dijon mustard

3 teaspoons vinegar or lemon juice

1 cup oil (corn, vegetable, olive or combination)

Place egg, mustard and vinegar (or lemon juice) in a blender; whirl until well blended. With blender running, very slowly add oil until thick. Season, if desired, with salt and pepper. Place in a covered container and refrigerate until ready to use.

MUSTARD-DILL SAUCE

Try this flavorful sauce with fresh cooked asparagus, tender green beans or grilled fish.

1 hard-boiled egg

1 whole raw egg

1 tablespoon Dijon mustard

1½ teaspoons white wine vinegar

1 teaspoon sugar

salt and freshly ground pepper

2 tablespoons fresh dill or 1½ teaspoons dried dill

2 tablespoons minced fresh parsley

½–¾ cup olive oil

lemon juice

Place hard-boiled egg yolk, raw egg, Dijon mustard, vinegar, sugar, dill, parsley, salt and pepper in a blender. Whirl until smooth. Slowly add oil until thick. Season with additional salt; pepper and add a squeeze of lemon juice if desired. Chill, covered.

REMOULADE SAUCE

This tangy mayonnaise-based sauce goes equally well with steamed artichokes, boiled shrimp or grilled salmon.

1 cup homemade (see recipe) or good quality mayonnaise

1 tablespoon finely chopped scallions

1 teaspoon dried basil

1 large clove garlic, minced

1 teaspoon dried tarragon

1 tablespoon minced fresh parsley

1 tablespoon Dijon mustard

1 teaspoon dillweed

1 teaspoon well-chopped capers

1 large dill pickle, finely chopped

anchovy paste

salt and pepper

Combine all ingredients in a bowl or blender, adding anchovy paste to taste. Adjust seasonings and add more herbs or scallions if needed. Refrigerate a few hours to blend flavors. Serve cold or at room temperature.

WISCONSIN BEER BATTER

For a truly authentic Wisconsin Friday Night Fish Fry, serve with homemade cole slaw and oven-baked potato fries.

1 cup flour

1 teaspoon baking powder

1½ teaspoons salt

1 tablespoon oil

1 cup stale beer

½–1 teaspoon Tabasco

peanut oil

flour

1 pound firm-fleshed fish (whitefish, lake perch, pike, muskie)

Mustard-Dill Sauce (see recipe)

Sift dry ingredients into a bowl. Make a well in the center and add the oil, beer and Tabasco. Whisk until smooth.

Pat fish dry with paper towels. Heat oil in deep skillet. Lightly sprinkle fish with flour and dip in batter. Drain off excess and place in hot fat—turn when golden. Remove and drain on paper towels and serve immediately with lemon wedges and Mustard-Dill Sauce.

Serves 2

WALLEYED PIKE VERACRUZ

A variation on the traditional Mexican dish, but instead of red snapper we feature Wisconsin's popular walleyed pike.

⅔ cup onions, chopped

4 cloves garlic, minced

1 tablespoon olive oil

2 fresh or canned jalapeño peppers, seeded and cut in slivers

1 16-ounce can Italian tomatoes, undrained and chopped coarsely

¼ teaspoon salt

½ teaspoon sugar

¼ teaspoon cinnamon

⅛ teaspoon ground cloves

1 tablespoon fresh lime juice

½ cup pimento-stuffed olives, halved

2 teaspoons capers

2 tablespoons fresh coriander, minced (optional)

2 pounds walleye fillets

lime wedges

Sauté onion and garlic in oil until soft. Add peppers, tomatoes with liquid, salt, sugar, cinnamon, cloves and lime juice. Cover and simmer 10 minutes. Stir in olives, capers and coriander. Add fish, if fillets are different thicknesses, place the largest in first—cook 1–2 minutes and add rest. Cover and poach for 15 minutes per inch of thickness.

Remove cover, place fish in platter and keep warm. Turn up heat on liquid and reduce sauce until slightly thick, 2–4 minutes. Spoon over fillets and serve at once with lime wedges.

Serves 3–4

FRESH TROUT WITH SPINACH STUFFING

For a sparkling and elegant spring dinner, serve this entree with homemade bread, braised leeks, a watercress salad and a strawberry-rhubarb tart.

1 whole trout, cleaned and boned with head and tail intact (approximately 1½ pounds)

1 small onion, minced

6 tablespoons butter

½ pound fresh spinach, steamed, drained, squeezed dry and finely chopped

3 slices bread, crusts removed, finely crumbled

½ cup minced parsley

½ teaspoon dried tarragon

salt and freshly ground pepper

1 egg, beaten

½ cup dry white wine

½ cup heavy cream

1½–2 tablespoons flour

Sauté onion in 2 tablespoons butter until soft; remove and place in a bowl. Add cooked spinach, bread crumbs, parsley, tarragon, salt, pepper and egg; blend well.

Stuff filling into trout and secure opening with skewers. Place in baking dish, pour in wine and cover with 2 tablespoons butter and foil. Bake in 450 degree oven. Calculate cooking time based on 10 minutes per inch of thickness. Remove when fish flakes easily. Place on a warm platter.

Add cream to pan, boil and reduce mixture by half. (Whisk in flour, stirring constantly, for a thick sauce.) Melt remaining 2 tablespoons butter and pour over trout.

Serves 2

SALMON AND AROMATIC VEGETABLES BAKED IN PARCHMENT PAPER

Serve with rice pilaf or baby new potatoes for a special dinner.

1 salmon fillet (about ¾ pound) cut in half, or 2 salmon steaks

6 julienne mushrooms

1 tablespoon lemon juice

6 tablespoons butter

1 tablespoon shallots, chopped

½ cup dry white wine

½ cup chicken stock

1 carrot, cut into matchsticks about 3 inches long

1 small stalk celery, cut into matchsticks about 3 inches long

1 tablespoon flour

½ teaspoon Dijon mustard

1 tablespoon grated lemon rind

1 tablespoon fresh dill, chopped

salt and white pepper to taste

large dash cayenne

parchment paper

Toss the mushrooms in lemon juice. In a saucepan melt 1 tablespoon butter, add the mushrooms and shallots, and sauté until the moisture has evaporated. Remove mushroom mixture and set aside.

To the pan, add wine and stock. Bring to a boil, add carrots and cook 2 minutes. Add celery and continue to cook for an additional minute. Strain vegetables from stock and set aside both in separate containers. In the same saucepan make roux by melting 1 tablespoon butter and adding the flour. Whisk constantly for a minute, add the reserved stock and 2 tablespoons butter, whisk, add the mustard, whisk again, and if sauce is *very* thick add more chicken stock. Add reserved vegetables, lemon rind, dill, mushrooms, salt, pepper and cayenne to taste. Melt remaining butter and set aside.

Cut parchment paper into two 15-inch squares. Fold in half and with scissors cut into heart shapes. Paint one side of paper with butter, leaving a 1-inch dry border. Salt and pepper salmon lightly and place on one side of the paper's fold. Spoon half of the vegetable mixture over salmon and fold over other half of paper. Crimp edges together by folding over twice. Repeat procedures with second parchment piece.

Butter a cookie sheet and place enclosed salmon on top. Bake 12–15 minutes in a preheated 400 degree oven.

The vegetables can be prepared and the packets assembled earlier in the day and placed in the oven just before serving.

Serves 2

LAKE PERCH FILLETS WITH ROSEMARY

The secret to this lightly fried fish is the fresh bread crumb coating. To achieve the fluffy texture, be sure only fresh white or French bread (crusts removed) is used.

1 pound lake perch fillets

½ cup flour

salt and pepper

2 teapoons paprika

1½ tablespoons dried rosemary, crumbled

2 eggs

2 cups fresh bread crumbs (5 slices fresh bread whirled in a blender)

¼ cup (or as needed) peanut oil

3 tablespoons (or as needed) butter

lemon wedges

Remoulade Sauce

Mix flour, salt, pepper, paprika and rosemary on wax paper. Dredge fillets in seasoned mixture and shake off any excess. Place on clean sheet of wax paper.

Beat eggs in shallow dish. Place crumbs on another sheet of wax paper. Dip each fillet in beaten egg then in bread crumbs, pressing with your hands to make sure crumbs adhere. (Coated fish can be chilled 30 minutes, if desired.)

Heat oil and butter until hot. Fry fillets a few at a time, about 30 seconds or until golden brown; regulate heat. Add more oil and butter as needed. Drain on paper towels and immediately transfer to heated platter. Garnish with lemon wedges and serve with Remoulade Sauce.

Serves 2

SUMMER

Wisconsin's beautiful summer days are as varied as its vistas. From the bluffs of the great Mississippi to the rolling hills of farm country to the jeweled lakes of the North Country, there are innumerable opportunities to revel in the season and its joys. And the bounty of the growing season is everywhere— from the smallest truck farm selling its produce at the local farmers market to the largest dairy farm. Backyard gardens, roadside stands, grocery stores and supermarkets overflow with Wisconsin-grown products. Menus turn toward salads, fruits and cheeses, vegetables of all varieties, grilled meats, and fruit-laden desserts. It is a time when meals themselves often move outdoors, from the proverbial backyard barbecue to the ubiquitous picnic—a time when culinary tastes range from the casual to the gourmet.

BERRY TIME

Wisconsin is a berry state, from the first harvest of strawberries in June to the wild blackberries still ripe for the picking in late summer. In between, there are raspberries, gooseberries, loganberries and blueberries. Many of these berries grow wild around the state, others are commercially harvested, and most are abundantly available at farmers markets and small groceries throughout the berry season.

The first local strawberries of the season are generally not as succulent as later harvests. Those exposed to longer periods of warmer weather produce sweeter fruits. Round berries generally have a better flavor than the larger, conical-shaped ones. The smaller varieties (wild or alpine), which are considered juicier and sweeter, are rarely marketed, but worth searching out. They prove that bigger is not necessarily better when it comes to strawberries.

Leave the hulls on until you're ready to use the berries, and make sure to check for and remove any moldy fruit, since the decay will spread rapidly to others in contact. Wash strawberries in a pan of water, rather than directly under running water, since they bruise easily.

Dip unhulled fresh strawberries in sour cream and brown sugar, and serve with wine and cheese or fruit soup. For an elegant touch, serve berries with a dash of sherry or your favorite liqueur. Add them to whipped cream for a dessert topping or a filling for crepes.

Perhaps the most exquisite summer berry is the raspberry. While they grow in three varieties, red, black and gold, it is the deep-red garnet raspberry that is the most favored. The season varies across the state from July through early August, and while raspberries are relatively expensive in the stores, pick-your-own farms usually offer a reasonable price. Bring shallow containers, perhaps cookie sheets, to prevent crushing your valuable bounty before you get it home.

Raspberries are marvelous plain, in pastries, souffles and toppings. But there are other uses, too, such as raspberry vinegar, that opens up all sorts of possibilities. The vinegar is made with puréed juice (from the not-so-perfect berries), vinegar and sugar. After a period of fermentation, it makes a concentrate used for wonderfully quenching drinks. When mixed with a fruity olive or nut oil, raspberry vinegar makes a special dressing for delicate fruit and salad greens.

If you end up with more strawberries, raspberries or blackberries than you can eat, just freeze them for later use. Clean, sort and spread them on cookie sheets and freeze them three to four hours until they're firm. Store them in plastic containers to prevent crushing. Don't be put off by the fuss of putting up a few jars of jams and jellies. Consult a grandmother —or a standard cookbook—and find out just how easy it is.

Raspberry 'n cream tulip cups make a refreshing summer dessert.

FRESH BOSTON LETTUCE AND STRAWBERRY SALAD

For a variation of this salad, plus dazzling color, add a few fresh blueberries, toasted walnuts and a sprinkling of fresh chives or tarragon.

1 large head Boston lettuce, washed
½ pint box of strawberries, sliced

VINAIGRETTE:
2 tablespoons fresh lemon juice
4 tablespoons olive or salad oil
1 teaspoon sugar
1 teaspoon salt
freshly ground pepper
¼–½ teaspoon dried tarragon

Combine juice, oil, sugar, salt, pepper, and tarragon in jar and shake well.

To assemble: Arrange whole leaves of Boston lettuce on salad plates. Arrange slices of strawberries decoratively on top of lettuce (about 2–4 berries per plate). Drizzle dressing on top of salad and serve at room temperature.

Serves 6

RASPBERRY MOUSSE

A perfect, easy-to-make dessert for those elegant summer dinners.

1 quart fresh raspberries
1⅓ cups powdered sugar
2 cups heavy cream
¼ teaspoon salt
1 teaspoon vanilla (Grand Marnier,
   Triple Sec, or Crème de Cassis
   may be substituted)

Wash berries; add sugar and let stand 1 hour. Reserve ½ cup of berries for decorating. Mash and strain rest through a fine sieve. Whip cream, add salt and vanilla. Fold into strained berry liquid. Pour into two refrigerator trays or metal cake pans or molds. Cover with plastic wrap and freeze mixture for 4 hours or overnight. Unmold or scoop onto dessert plates. Garnish with reserved berries. Serve immediately.

Serves 6

RASPBERRY 'N CREAM TULIP CUPS

The filling and sauce may be made several days ahead. Assemble just an hour before serving to keep the phyllo crunchy.

8 sheets phyllo pastry
¼ pound butter (1 stick) melted
Cream Cheese Filling
Raspberry Sauce
Fresh raspberries

Place the first sheet of phyllo on work surface, cover remaining sheets with plastic wrap and damp towel at all times (the dough dries out fast, and once it begins to crack and tear, it is impossible to work with). Carefully brush pastry sheet lightly with melted butter. Layer second sheet of phyllo on top and continue layering and buttering, four sheets in total. Cut layered phyllo into thirds horizontally and vertically, ending with nine squares. Press each square into buttered 2½ inch muffin tins pressing the bottom flat and folding excess dough to create a petal effect on sides. Continue to butter, layer, cut and fit remaining four phyllo sheets. Bake in bottom third of 345 degree oven for about 12 minutes until lightly golden brown. Fill with about 3 tablespoons of filling, top with fresh raspberries and serve with raspberry sauce.

CREAM CHEESE FILLING
8 ounces cream cheese, softened
4 tablespoons granulated sugar
1½ teaspoons grated lemon rind
2 teaspoons lemon juice
1 teaspoon grated orange rind
5 tablespoons Amaretto

In a bowl or food processor, combine cream cheese, sugar, lemon and orange. Combine well, slowly add Amaretto. Refrigerate until ready to use.

RASPBERRY SAUCE
1 pint (2 cups) fresh raspberries
   (or frozen)
¼ cup sugar or to taste, depending on
   sweetness of berries
1 tablespoon fresh lemon juice
1 tablespoon cornstarch mixed with
   3 tablespoons berry juice or water
3 tablespoons kirsch

Purée raspberries in food processor or blender. Press through sieve to remove seeds. In small sauce pan add purée and sugar, bring to boil, reduce heat. Add lemon juice and cornstarch mixture, whisk until well combined and smooth. Remove from heat and stir in kirsch.

Serves 18

RASPBERRY VINEGAR

This is a good way to use the not-so-perfect berries.

3 pints fresh raspberries, cleaned
3 cups cider vinegar
sugar

Place raspberries in crock or jar. Pour in vinegar and allow to stand overnight. Next day strain and measure juice. For each pint of juice formed, add 2 cups sugar, boil 10 minutes. Pour hot concentrate into sterilized jars and seal, or store in refrigerator for several weeks.

(When using sweetened frozen raspberries, vary ingredients to 2¼ cups cider vinegar and 1½ cups sugar for each pint of juice.)

RASPBERRY SHRUB

A quenching drink and unique cocktail.

2–3 tablespoons Raspberry Vinegar
½ cup club soda or water

Mix vinegar and soda or water and pour over ice cubes. Add sprig of mint and serve. To serve as cocktail, add small amount of vodka to each glass.

STRAWBERRY ALMOND TART

The rich cookie crust for this tart can be speedily made in a food processor. Place all the ingredients in bowl and process 1–2 seconds until it resembles coarse meal. Flatten into a circle, wrap and chill.

3 egg yolks

½ cup sugar

6 tablespoons unsalted butter

½ cup ground almonds

3–4 tablespoons kirsch

1-nine-inch Rich Tart Crust, partially baked

1 quart strawberries

½ cup apricot preserves

¼ cup sliced almonds, lightly toasted

Preheat oven to 350 degrees. Beat egg yolks and ¼ cup sugar until they form a ribbon. In separate bowl beat remaining ¼ cup sugar and butter until smooth. Combine two mixtures and stir until smooth. Add ½ cup ground almonds and 1 tablespoon kirsch (to taste). Pour into partially baked crust. Bake for 10 minutes or until cream is set. Watch closely so surface does not burn. Cool completely.

Meanwhile, wash, hull and halve strawberries. Place on paper towels to dry. When ready to assemble, arrange strawberries, cut side down, attractively on cooled almond cream. Melt apricot preserves and rub through strainer, add 1–2 tablespoons kirsch. Carefully brush glaze over tart, then sprinkle with toasted almonds.

RICH TART CRUST
½ cup unsalted butter

1½ cups sifted flour

2 tablespoons sugar

¼ teaspoon salt

3 tablespoons ground almonds

2 teaspoons grated fresh lemon rind

1 egg

1–2 tablespooons cold milk (if necessary)

Soften butter slightly by tapping with rolling pin. Mix flour, sugar, salt, ground almonds and grated lemon rind in large bowl. Make a well in center. Add butter in slices to the well, then add egg. Make paste of butter and egg and gradually incorporate dry ingredients. Gather dough into ball, add cold milk if too dry. Wrap in waxed paper and chill for two hours or overnight. Roll out between two pieces of waxed paper, fit into 9-inch pie pan and bake 20 minutes or until crust just starts to turn golden.

Serves 10

CHILLED STRAWBERRY SOUP

Serve this as a first course followed by grilled fish or at a light summer luncheon.

2 pints fresh strawberries, cleaned and hulled

1 cup orange juice

1¼ teaspoons instant tapioca

¼ teaspoon cinnamon

¼ teaspoon ground allspice

½ cup sugar

1 teaspoon grated lemon peel

1 tablespoon lemon juice

1 cup buttermilk

Purée strawberries in food processor or blender. Strain into saucepan and add orange juice. In a small bowl mix tapioca with 4 tablespoons of puréed strawberry mixture. Add to saucepan with allspice and cinnamon. Heat, stirring constantly until mixture comes to boil. Cook until thickened. Remove from heat. Pour into large bowl, add sugar, lemon peel, lemon juice and buttermilk and blend well. Cover and chill at least 8 hours. Taste and add more lemon flavoring, if needed. Serve with fresh berry or lemon slice.

Serves 6

CHOCOLATE RASPBERRY ROULADE

An elegant presentation with a unique combination of flavors—chocolate, apricot and raspberry.

¼ pound semisweet chocolate

2 tablespoons strong black coffee

4 eggs, separated

⅔ cup brown sugar

⅓ cup ground almonds

Chocolate Buttercream

½ cup apricot preserves

1–1½ cups fresh raspberries (1–10 oz. pkg. frozen raspberries, well drained, may be substituted)

Preheat oven to 375 degrees. Butter a 10″×15″ baking sheet. Fit with wax paper and butter again. Melt chocolate and coffee in double boiler. Beat egg yolks with brown sugar, slowly add melted chocolate mixture and beat well. Stir in ground almonds. Beat egg whites until stiff and fold into egg yolk-chocolate mixture. Spoon into prepared pan and level surface. Bake for 15 minutes or until cake is just firm to touch. Remove to cooling rack and cover roulade with clean damp cloth and set aside until cold.

CHOCOLATE BUTTERCREAM
5 ounces unsalted butter

1 cup powdered sugar

1 egg yolk

2 teaspoons sugar

2 teaspoons strong coffee

1½ ounces semisweet chocolate

¼ teaspoon almond extract

Melt chocolate with coffee in double boiler, set aside. Cream butter, add egg yolk, sugar, and almond extract. Blend in chocolate mixture. Add powdered sugar slowly, beating until very smooth and fluffy.

To assemble: Place roulade on waxed paper that has been sprinkled with powdered sugar. Remove baking paper. Thinly spread apricot preserves over cake. Spread buttercream over this and sprinkle with raspberries. Roll up long side, carefully and tightly, like jelly roll. Place seam side down on serving platter and chill at least 1 hour before serving. Serve plain, dusted with powdered sugar, or with Raspberry Sauce on the side.

Serves 12

✦

SOUP'S ON

Just when climbing temperatures chase even the most enthusiastic cook out of the kitchen, the garden produces an abundance of perfect soup ingredients: vine-ripened tomatoes, summer squash, peppers, beans, cucumbers, corn and fruits. And while soups win praises all year around for simplicity and versatility, quick, no-fuss, cold soups really shine as part of a summer menu. More than a catch-all for extra produce, they can be exciting dishes that capture all the freshness of the season.

Like any soup, cold soup relies on a good base. If your recipe calls for stock or broth, don't be tempted to use bouillon cubes—they're loaded with salt and have an overpowering chemical taste, especially cold. A canned stock is better than bouillon, and for most cold soups we recommend it even over homemade stock, which contains a natural gelatin that causes cold soups to jell.

Vegetables are the main ingredient in most cold soups, but exciting variations include seafood, chicken, duck and fruit. Always use the best fresh ingredients available. Rely on your garden's bounty or a farmers market for inspiration. If you have bushels of tomatoes but not enough peppers for a certain recipe, improvise— often this can be the beginning of another equally exciting cold soup. You can turn simple left-over vegetables into a satisfying cold melange by puréeing them and adding herbs and enough cream to make them smooth.

A blender produces the smoothest, silkiest soups, but a food mill or fine sieve will do. If your soup is too thick, thin it out with milk, yogurt, cream or buttermilk. If it's too thin, add puréed thickeners, either more vegetables or potatoes or rice. It's best to prepare the soup in advance to give the flavors plenty of time to develop and blend while chilling. Chilling tends to mute seasoning flavors, so over-seasoning is the rule. Be sure to taste your soup just before serving. A last-minute sprinkling of curry powder, fresh dill, mint, tarragon, chives or parsley will turn it into something special.

Present your soup with style. Have the individual bowls iced, or rest a tureen in a bowl of cracked ice. An array of garnishes adds room for creativity—homemade croutons, crumbled bacon, toasted sesame seeds or nuts, grated radishes or carrots, slivered peppers, sliced lemons or limes, diced cucumbers or chopped fresh herbs.

As an elegant first course or as a light main dish, simple and refreshing cold soup lets you keep your cool while enjoying summer's fresh flavors.

Soups that look as refreshing as they taste, (top to bottom) seafood gazpacho, fresh pea and curried cream of red pepper.

ICED CREAM OF PARSLEY SOUP

One of our favorite soups—an elegant choice for a dinner party or fancy picnic. The base is similar to vichyssoise, but the large amount of parsley adds a new flavor twist.

3 finely chopped leeks

2 finely chopped medium onions

2 tablespoons butter

1 bay leaf

4 cups chicken stock

5 medium potatoes, peeled and sliced

1 tablespoon salt

3 cups heavy cream

1 tablespoon Worcestershire sauce

2 cups chopped parsley, tightly packed

Sauté leeks and onions in butter. Add bay leaf, 3 cups stock and potatoes. Cover and simmer 35–40 minutes or until vegetables are tender. Remove bay leaf. Purée in batches. Refrigerate. When cold, stir in cream and season with Worcestershire sauce, salt and pepper. Purée the parsley with the remaining 1 cup stock. Add to the soup mixture, stir and refrigerate overnight.

Serves 10–12

CURRIED CREAM OF RED PEPPER SOUP

For a bit of the Southwest, serve this with fresh, hot tortillas, an avocado-tomato salad, grilled beef and Margaritas.

½ cup chopped onions

2 teaspoons curry powder

4 tablespoons butter

3 large fresh red bell peppers, chopped

2½ cups chicken stock

3 tablespoons raw white rice

1–1½ cups heavy cream

salt and freshly ground pepper

1 recipe Salsa

In a large saucepan sauté the onions and curry powder in the butter until soft, 2–3 minutes. Lower heat and add peppers, cook 3–4 minutes more. Add stock and rice, cover and simmer 15 minutes or until rice is cooked and peppers are very soft. Cool; purée in a blender or food processor (press through a fine sieve if desired). Add cream and season. Chill 8 hours or overnight. Taste and add more curry, salt and pepper if needed. Serve with a generous dollop of salsa in each bowl.

SALSA

6–8 firm, ripe tomatoes

1 green pepper, chopped

1 small onion, chopped

1 clove garlic, minced

1 tablespoon fresh coriander, minced

1 or more jalapeño peppers, minced and seeded

salt, freshly ground pepper, oregano

Place onions and garlic in a food processor and chop coarsely. (Can also be chopped by hand.) Remove to a bowl. Process peppers and tomatoes in the same manner. Add to onion-garlic mixture; mix in coriander. Salsa should have a course texture, not soupy. Add a dash of oregano, salt and pepper. Chill thoroughly.

Serves 12–14

COLD CORN AND ZUCCHINI SOUP

This late summer harvest soup has lots of flavor. Purée it until smooth, then add some cooked corn kernels for texture if you wish.

4 ears fresh corn

¼ cup (½ stick) butter

2 tablespoons olive oil

1 large onion, minced

2 cloves garlic, minced

4 fresh tomatoes, peeled, seeded and finely chopped, or 2 cups canned Italian plum tomatoes, finely chopped, and their liquid

4 cups beef stock

5 thin zucchini, cut into 1-inch slices

3 tablespoons minced fresh basil, or 1 tablespoon dried basil

5 tablespoons freshly grated Parmesan cheese

1 small dried hot chili pepper, or ½ teaspoon dried red pepper flakes

salt and freshly ground black pepper

1¾ cups whipping cream

Cook corn in boiling water until tender, about 5 minutes. Drain and cool.

Melt butter and oil in large saucepan, add onions and cook for 10 minutes. Add garlic and cook for 2 minutes. Stir in tomatoes, stock, zucchini, basil, cheese and red pepper. Cook until zucchini is tender but still slightly crispy.

Purée until smooth. Blend in corn, taste and season with salt and pepper. Transfer to a large covered container and chill. Blend in cream and adjust seasoning. Garnish with chopped fresh parsley or chives.

Serves 18

FRESH PEA SOUP

Serve icy cold for a luncheon or a first course when you have a bumper crop of peas.

2 tablespoons butter

¾ cup chopped onion

½ cup sliced carrots

1 medium potato, peeled and chopped

2 cups shredded lettuce (Boston, romaine, or iceberg)

4 cups chicken stock

1 teaspoon sugar

2 cups shelled peas

1 cup half & half, or ½ cup cream and ½ cup milk

¾ cup sour cream

1 teaspoon salt

pepper to taste

dash cayenne

fresh chives or scallion greens

In a large saucepan sauté the onions and carrots in the butter for about 3 minutes. Add the potato and continue to sauté another 4–6 minutes, until the vegetables are tender but not browned. Add lettuce and gently braise for an additional 4 minutes. Add sugar, stock and 1 teaspoon salt; bring to a boil.

Reduce heat and cook 5–10 minutes. Add peas and cook until they are very tender. Cool soup and purée in a blender until very smooth. Add half & half and sour cream. Season to taste and chill. Serve garnished with chopped chives, sliced scallion greens or fresh mint.

Serves 6

HUNGARIAN SQUASH SOUP

For a truly Hungarian flavor, substitute several sprinklings of paprika for the Tabasco.

3 cups peeled, sliced yellow summer squash

½ teaspoon salt

1 tablespoon vinegar

1 tablespoon butter

1 onion, minced

2 eggs

1 cup sour cream

dash of Tabasco

½ cup chopped fresh dill (or 1 tablespoon dried dill weed)

In a kettle, place squash, salt, vinegar and just enough water to cover. Cook for 8–10 minutes or until tender. Meanwhile, in a skillet melt the butter and sauté the onion until translucent. Purée contents of kettle together with the onion, eggs, sour cream, Tabasco and dill. Chill and adjust seasonings.

Serves 6

SEAFOOD GAZPACHO

This version of gazpacho, made with shrimp, is a refreshing change from the usual, and it's substantial enough to be the main course on those hot nights when you don't feel like cooking.

2 cups fresh white bread crumbs (made from fresh bread whirled in a blender)

3 cloves garlic, minced

1 cucumber, peeled, seeded and cut into ¼-inch pieces

2 sweet red or green peppers, cored, seeded and finely chopped

3 jalapeño peppers, cored, seeded and finely chopped

1 medium red onion, finely chopped

2 cups chicken stock

2 14-ounce cans Italian tomatoes, drained (or the equivalent fresh)

3 cups tomato juice (use some of the drained tomato liquid)

½ cup fresh lime juice

½ cup olive oil

2 teaspoons ground cumin seed

salt and freshly ground pepper

1 pound cooked shrimp, cut up

1 or 2 ripe avocadoes, diced

Combine bread crumbs and garlic; set aside. In a large bowl mix the cucumber, peppers, onion, stock, tomatoes and juice. Stir in lime juice, oil and bread crumbs mixture. Purée only half the soup in a blender and stir back into bowl. Season with cumin, salt and pepper. Refrigerate until cold. Stir in shrimp and avocado. Chill again before serving.

Serves 18–20

Tart and juicy, they're ripe
for more than just pies

"PIE" CHERRIES

When it comes to cherries, Wisconsin is abundantly blessed—Door County is one of the nation's leaders in the production of this favorite summer treat. While sweet cherries thrive in warm climates, mostly on the West Coast, the tart, sour "pie" cherries do best along the cool, sandy shores of Lake Michigan. They are rounder, with a softer texture, and their exceptionally juicy, tart flavor is perfect for pies, tarts, puddings, sauces, jellies, syrup and breads.

Almost without fail, the cherry trees burst into delicate white blossoms within two weeks of Memorial Day, heralding the arrival of summer; by mid-July, the trees become laden with fruit. Most of Wisconsin's orchards are owned by small growers who only produce enough to sell to local canning companies. But near the end of July and into August, many orchards allow you the fun of picking your own. If you prefer less work, but still desire the unmistakable taste of fresh cherries, stop at the plentiful roadside stands. There are many opportunities to buy pies, breads, jellies and jams at these markets, also.

Growing cherries at home is also an option. Because the trees are self-pollinating, you'll need only one and you're in business. North Star, a hardy, small popular variety with bright fruit that ripens early in the season, is especially suited to the far northern regions. Another small tree is the English Morello, which bears medium-size, dark red cherries, firm and very tart, perfect for cooking and canning. The medium-to-large Montmorency is the standard commercial cherry tree, loaded with brilliant red fruit. If you don't have the garden space for one of these, you may want to consult your local nursery about dwarf or bush varieties.

Cherries with stems keep better, but if you plan to use them within a day or two, stemmed cherries are a wiser buy. Store cherries, unwashed, in the refrigerator, where they will keep for several days. To prepare, first soak them in cold water for a few hours to firm the flesh and then use a cherry pitter to remove the stone. Raw sour cherries can be frozen or canned, either plain with a light sugar syrup, or sweetened and spiced for preserves, jellies, jams or a ready-made pie filling. The shelf life of canned cherries is between one and three years; frozen cherries keep for one year.

We've included some traditional (cherry pie) and not so traditional (cherry soup) recipes for this great Wisconsin fruit.

It's hard to beat the simple goodness of old-fashioned cherry pie made with Door County's tart cherries.

CHILLED CHERRY SOUP

A rich, delicate soup to be served icy cold on those especially hot days of summer.

1 pound tart cherries
⅓ cup sugar
3 cups Riesling wine
⅛ teaspoon powered cinnamon
grated rind of 1 lemon
juice of two lemons
¼ cup brandy
2½ cups sour cream
sour cream
nutmeg

Pit the cherries reserving pits and stems and juice. In small sauce pan combine pits, stems, juice, sugar and wine; bring to boil and simmer for 5 minutes. Strain liquid into clean sauce pan. Add cinnamon, lemon rind, and juice. Bring to boil, add cherries and any extra juice. Bring back to boil, remove from heat. Allow to cool slightly and stir in brandy.

In blender, add half of the cherry mixture and half the sour cream, blend until smooth. Repeat with a second batch. Serve well chilled with a dollop of sour cream and a grate of fresh nutmeg.

Serves 6–8

ROAST DUCK WITH CHERRY SAUCE

For a sparkling clear sauce to accompany this duck, thoroughly strain the stockport mixture before adding the cherry liquid.

1 4–4½ pound duck
salt and pepper
orange juice
1 pound sour pitted cherries (reserve liquid)
grated rind of ½ orange
⅓ cup sugar
generous sprinkling of freshly grated
*   nutmeg*
½ cup port
1 tablespoon currant jelly
1¼ cups stock (made from giblets, 1 bay leaf,
*   ½ teaspoon thyme)*
2 tablespoons butter
2 teaspoons cornstarch mixed with
*   1 tablespoon stock*

Preheat oven to 425 degrees. Clean and rinse duck. Prick skin all over. Salt and pepper inside and out and rub skin with some orange juice. Truss and place in a roasting pan. Bake 15 minutes to brown slightly. Reduce heat to 350 degrees and continue roasting 1 hour for medium rare and 1 hour 15 minutes for well done. Remove fat from bottom of pan frequently.

Meanwhile soak cherries, their liquid, the orange rind, sugar, nutmeg, and ¼ cup port for 30 minutes. When duck is done, remove to hot platter, cover with foil and keep warm. Discard all fat from pan, except 1 tablespoon. Place over high heat and add stock and ¼ cup port. Boil, scraping bottom and reduce by half. Remove cherries from marinade and set aside. Pour cherry liquid in pan and cook down slightly. Whisk in butter, currant jelly, then cornstarch mixture. Cook over medium heat until slightly thick, add cherries and heat through. Taste and adjust seasonings. Serve in bowl to accompany sliced roasted duck.

Serves 4

CHERRY PIE

Another trusted recipe from Madison's "Pie Queen," Cindy Edwards. She suggests the pie be served cold, but if you can't wait, serve it hot anyway—but cool it with homemade vanilla ice cream.

PASTRY
unbaked 9″ bottom crust and strips
for top crust

FILLING
4 cups fresh or frozen cherries
1 cup sugar (for fresh cherries and ⅔ cup
*   sugar for frozen cherries)*
3 tablespoons instant tapioca
½ teaspoon almond extract
dash salt
1 tablespoon fresh lemon juice
2 tablespoons butter

In large bowl mix together cherries, sugar, tapioca, almond extract and salt. Let sit 5 to 10 minutes. Roll out reserved pie crust. Cut into 1-inch strips with pastry wheel. Pour filling into prepared pie shell, drizzle with lemon juice, dot with butter. Weave pastry strips over the filling, trim long strips and tuck in, crimp edges. Brush with sugar and water glaze or milk. Bake in preheated 375 degree oven 60–75 minutes until filling bubbles in the center.

Serves 8

CHERRY PECAN BREAD

During the height of cherry season, bake several loaves of this bread and freeze for later use as holiday gifts.

1 egg, room temperature

6 ounces tart cherries, pitted and quartered

1 cup sugar

½ teaspoon grated lemon rind

2 tablespoons butter, melted

½ cup cherry juice

¼ cup orange juice

2 cups flour

3 teaspoons baking powder

¼ teaspoon baking soda

1 teaspoon salt

1 cup lightly toasted pecans, chopped

Grease pan and preheat oven to 350 degrees. In large bowl beat egg, add cherries and stir in the sugar, lemon rind and melted butter. Pour in cherry and orange juice. Sift flour, baking powder, baking soda and salt together. Add to cherry liquid mixture a spoonful at a time, blend together thoroughly. Stir in chopped nuts.

Pour into the prepared pan and level with spoon. Bake about 1¼ hours or until crust is well-browned and a wooden toothpick inserted in center of loaf comes out clean.

Remove from the oven, let rest 10 minutes and remove from the pan to a wire rack to cool. Wrap with foil or plastic wrap. This bread is better when seasoned for a day or two before serving.

Makes one 8½″ × 4½″ loaf

LORA BRODY'S CHOCOLATE CHERRY TORTE

One of the best chocolate cakes available. We changed the recipe slightly adding more chocolate and substituting frozen Door County cherries for canned ones.

3 tablespoons bread crumbs

16 ounces frozen cherries (or 1 16-ounce can pitted)

7 ounces semi-sweet chocolate

12 tablespoons butter

⅔ cup sugar

3 eggs

1 teaspoon vanilla

½ teaspoon almond extract

½ cup almonds, ground

⅔ cup flour

2 tablespoons powdered sugar

8 ounces almond paste

Preheat oven to 350 degrees. Butter a 9-inch springform pan. Add bread crumbs to pan and shake. Set aside. Drain cherries and set aside. In small sauce pan add chocolate and set over water on warm burner until melted. Set aside. In large mixing bowl add butter and sugar. Blend with mixer until light and creamy. Add two of the eggs, beat well. Add the last egg. Beat in vanilla and almond extracts. Stir in chocolate and blend well. Mix in almonds and flour. Pour into prepared pan and smooth top. Arrange drained cherries in circle covering entire surface, press in gently. Bake 50 minutes to 1 hour. Do not overbake; cake will be moist in center. Cool and remove from pan.

Place waxed paper on flat surface and sprinkle with powdered sugar. Work almond paste with your hands and rolling pin to make a flat, 9-inch circle. Pour some glaze on bottom surface of cake. Place almond paste circle on top. Pour additional glaze over top and spread sides and top smooth. Chill and add a second coating.

GLAZE
½ cup heavy cream
2 teaspoons dried espresso coffee granules
8 ounces semi-sweet chocolate

In small sauce pan add cream and coffee, bring to slow boil. Add chocolate, whisking until melted and smooth. Let cool briefly until spreadable.

Serves 8–10

CHERRY CLAFOUTIS
(French Cherry Pancake)

Serve this show-stopper pancake at your next brunch.

1 cup milk

2 tablespoons brandy

¼ cup sugar

3 eggs

2 teaspoons vanilla extract

⅔ cup sifted all-purpose flour

2 tablespoons melted butter

1 pound sour cherries

3 tablespoons sugar

powdered sugar

Place all ingredients except cherries and 3 tablespoons sugar in a blender and blend at high speed for 1 minute. Place one fourth of batter in buttered cast-iron two quart shallow casserole or skillet. (To prevent batter from sticking to the pan, put 1½ tablespoons butter in the skillet and place in the oven until it begins to bubble; swirl around the pan.) Place over low heat on stove burner for a minute or two to set batter on bottom of dish. Cover with cherries and sprinkle with reserved sugar. Pour on remaining batter; bake in preheated 400 degree oven for 30–45 minutes, or until puffed and golden brown. Sprinkle with powdered sugar and serve warm.

Serves 4–6

CHICKEN IN A BASKET

There are outdoor occasions that call for a little more elegance than hamburgers, pickles and potato salad. Such was the case for us on our first visit to the American Players Theatre near Spring Green. The lovely hillside setting of the outdoor stage and adjoining picnic grounds inspired a gourmet menu.

Needing something to please the young children in our group as well as the adults, we prepared a glazed roasted chicken. A fresh roaster was our choice, though capon and cornish hens can be prepared in the same way with very satisfying results. Making this dish a day early and refrigerating it brings out the full flavor and lessens the preparation time on the day of the outing. Our coriander rice salad, too, is more flavorful the next day; just add the currants at the last minute since they tend to get soggy.

A soup that can be carried in a thermos is ideal—ours was an iced tomato cream soup. It is important that the stock in this soup be homemade or canned; bouillon cubes don't do the job. They are chemical feasts overwhelmed with salt. Pack, separately, homemade croutons, toasted sesame seeds, grated radishes or carrots, slivered red or green peppers, diced cucumbers or minced fresh herbs to serve as garnish.

While you can prepare the green bean and walnut sauce early, combine them at your picnic site to keep the beans from getting mushy.

While getting food to a picnic in one piece can be a problem, we chose marzipan, a dense single-layer cake, rather than risking a smashed fruit tart. It is best to keep the fresh raspberry topping off this cake until it is time to serve it.

We packed our picnic and service in several baskets and an old picnic hamper. Befitting a gourmet picnic, we used the real thing—cloth—for the table and used colorful kitchen towels as napkins (they had already served to protect the wine glasses). Citronella candles prettied things up and warded off visiting insects.

When your special alfresco occasions call for special menus, just prepare these dishes a day early. It will make the event itself all the more fun.

A picnic feast—glazed roast chicken, green beans in walnut sauce, coriander rice salad and marzipan cake with fresh raspberry sauce.

ICED TOMATO CREAM SOUP

A terrific way to use up the plethora of tomatoes that seems to appear in the garden overnight.

1 tablespoon butter

1 medium onion, chopped

6 fresh tomatoes, peeled, seeded and chopped

½ cup chicken stock

½ teaspoon sugar

½ teaspoon dried thyme

½ teaspoon salt

¾ cup heavy cream

¼ cup sour cream

lime juice

salt and freshly ground pepper

sliced limes

Melt butter in skillet and add onions. Cover and sauté over low heat 15 minutes or until soft. Add tomatoes, stock, sugar, thyme and salt. Simmer, uncovered, for 10 minutes. Cool. Purée in blender or food processor with the heavy cream, sour cream and a sprinkling of lime juice. Force through a fine sieve. Taste and add salt, pepper and additional lime juice, if necessary. Chill. Serve with slices of lime.

Serves 6

CORIANDER RICE SALAD

This dish can be turned into a spectacular light summer entree with the addition of cooked sliced Chinese sausages or boiled shrimp.

3–4 cups cooked rice

1 cup French dressing (made with ⅓ cup vinegar, ⅔ cup oil, 1½ teaspoons dried tarragon or 1 tablespoon fresh, 1 small clove garlic, pressed)

¼ cup minced fresh parsley

1 onion, chopped fine

1 tablespoon currants, cooked in hot water 3 minutes and drained

2 tablespoons pinenuts or slivered almonds toasted in oil

1 tablespoon whole coriander seeds, simmered in water, about 15–20 minutes and drained

10 stuffed green olives, sliced

½ cup celery with leaves, finely chopped

1 green pepper, slivered finely

GARNISH

1 tomato, peeled, seeded, and cut into eighths

¾ cup cucumber, chopped

fresh basil leaves

lemon juice

Mix hot rice with French dressing, add parsley, onion, nuts, coriander, olives, celery and green pepper. Adjust seasoning with lemon juice, salt and pepper. Add currants just before serving, then garnish decoratively with cucumber, tomato and basil leaves. Serve at room temperature.

Serves 6–8

GREEN BEANS IN WALNUT SAUCE

Set aside 1 tablespoon walnuts when blending the sauce and sprinkle over the green beans for a crunchy texture.

1½ pounds fresh green beans

¾ cup scallions, including green tops, minced

3 tablespoons minced parsley

4 tablespoons minced fresh dill, or 1–1¼ teaspoons dried

3 tablespoons cider vinegar

3 ounces walnuts, coarsely chopped

½–¾ cup olive oil

salt and pepper

dill sprigs

Steam or gently cook beans in water until just tender and drain. In blender combine scallions, parsley, dill, vinegar, walnuts and ½ cup oil. Blend mixture until smooth, adding a little more oil if necessary. Season with salt and pepper. Pour over beans. Toss; chill for several hours. Bring back to room temperature to serve.

Serves 6

GLAZED ROASTING CHICKEN

For a truly elegant touch, accompany this chicken dish with an assortment of chutney's—apricot, mango or plum.

1 large roasting chicken (or 4 cornish hens or a capon)

4 slices thick bacon, cut in thin strips

3 tablespoons fresh parsley, chopped

1 tablespoon fresh chives, chopped

1 tablespoon fresh rosemary, chopped (or 1 teaspoon dried)

2 teaspoons fresh sage, chopped (or 1 teaspoon dried)

1 lemon, juiced

4 tablespoons butter

4 tablespoons apricot preserves

4 tablespoons sherry

2 tablespoons honey

Combine herbs and bacon and chop very fine. Set aside. To stuff chicken (Note: stuffing will go between bird's skin and flesh, not in its cavity), lift skin at the neck, slip your fingers under skin working downwards, loosening skin over breast and thighs as far as your fingers can reach. Push half of seasoned bacon-herb mixture under skin and down around bird's thighs and drumsticks. With your other hand smooth stuffing from outside. Push remaining stuffing under skin and onto breast and continue to pat down with your other hand. Secure bird's legs by tying together. Rub chicken with butter, place in shallow roasting pan. Sprinkle with salt and pepper. Roast in preheated 350-degree oven for 1 hour. After first 10 minutes of roasting baste with lemon juice and butter. Afterwards, baste chicken with pan juices every 10–20 minutes. While chicken is roasting, melt together in small saucepan apricot preserves, sherry and honey. Brush glaze on chicken, then return to oven, roasting an additional 25–35 minutes, basting frequently with glaze until golden brown.

Serves 6

MARZIPAN CAKE WITH FRESH RASPBERRY SAUCE

This is an all-time winner. If fresh raspberries are not available, substitute a cooked frozen raspberry sauce (recipe in "Berry" section).

¾ cup sugar

1 stick unsalted butter, room temperature

8 ounces almond paste

3 eggs

1 tablespoon kirsch

¼ teaspoon almond extract

½ cup flour

⅓ teaspoon baking powder

powdered sugar

Preheat oven to 350 degrees. Butter, line with waxed paper or parchment paper, and butter again an 8-inch round pan. Combine sugar, butter, and almond paste in mixing bowl and blend well. Beat in eggs, kirsch, and almond extract. Add flour and baking powder; beat until just mixed through. Do not overbeat. Bake until tester inserted in center of cake comes out clean, about 40–50 minutes. Let cool. Invert on serving platter and dust lightly with powdered sugar.

RASPBERRY SAUCE

2½ cups fresh raspberries

2 tablespoons sugar, or to suit your taste

kirsch, Grand Marnier, or other liqueur flavorings (optional)

Combine 2 cups raspberries with sugar in blender or food processor and purée. Press through sieve to remove seeds. Add dash of liqueur, if desired. Add remaining whole berries. Serve along with slice of marzipan cake.

Serves 8–10

It's far more than tomato sauce and pasta

FEASTING ITALIAN

From the Italians come some of the best loved and most imitated foods in the world. Even families without a trace of Italian ancestry can claim at least one prized recipe for spaghetti and meatballs or lasagna.

In Wisconsin Italian immigrants settled mainly in three sections of the state, Milwaukee's Brady Street area, Kenosha and the shores of Lake Superior near Hurley. For a look at how this group still celebrates its heritage and for a taste of genuine Italian cooking in all its variety, visit the outdoor summer Festa Italiana in Milwaukee.

In a traditional Italian meal several courses are offered, each of relatively equal size. An antipasto platter is served first that includes such items as olives, marinated mushrooms, peppers, anchovies, artichoke hearts, calamari (fried squid), sliced cold meats and cheeses. This course is served with crusty bread or breadsticks and light crisp white wines like Soave or Orvieto or light bodied reds, Bardolino, Valopolicella or Chianti.

Primo piatto, or the first course, is generally a clear or light soup such as *Zuppa Panese* (egg consomme), *minestra di funghi* (mushroom), *tortellini in brodo* (filled shells in broth) or a pasta dish. Pasta, Italian style, is made of one hundred percent semolina (a hard durum wheat) which makes the noodles quite firm. You can recreate this same kind in your own kitchen—a simple and fun dish the whole family will enjoy making. For extra flavor and color add a half cup of pureed, cooked vegetables to our basic recipe. Especially good are carrots, spinach, beets, tomatoes, roasted red peppers or mixed herbs. To fully appreciate the flavor of homemade pasta,

serve it simply with butter, freshly grated Romano or Parmesan cheese, and black pepper.

The second course, *secondo piatto,* is the equivalent of an entree—fish, poultry or meat (especially veal), typically accompanied by steamed fennel (a licorice-flavored root vegetable), sautéed zucchini, stuffed artichokes or eggplant.

Salad follows the entree, usually a dish of assertive greens—chicory, arugula, radicchio, romaine, endive or escarole. Use them sparingly because they are quite strong and somewhat bitter. Toss your salad with a simple vinaigrette, using imported extra virgin olive oil—it's strong and clear with a slight green color. As with any olive oil, always store it in a cool, dark place as exposure to light and heat will turn it rancid.

The finale of any Italian meal is usually very simple—fresh fruit, figs, pears, apples, sometimes macerated in sweet wines, a dish of gelato (a rich, egg custard) or a wedge of sharp cheese. For special occasions consider one of the rich cheesecakes Italians are famous for. They're often made with ricotta (a mild and creamy Italian version of cottage cheese.) Other tempting options are zabaglione (custard flavored with wine) and cannoli (fried cookie shells filled with ricotta, chocolate and candied fruit).

"Straw and hay" pasta in an Asiago cheese sauce and stuffed flank steak with a Marsala mushroom sauce team up in an authentically Italian meal.

MIXED SALAD
(Insalata Mista)

For a more colorful salad add julienne slices of sweet roasted red peppers, pitted marinated olives, capers and lightly toasted pine nuts.

1 large fennel bulb, thinly sliced

*1½–2 quarts assorted cleaned salad greens,
   torn in small pieces*

1 tablespoon chives, chopped

1 small red onion, thinly sliced

VINAIGRETTE

juice of ½ lemon

*4 tablespoons balsamic vinegar or red wine
   vinegar*

1 clove garlic, minced

freshly ground pepper

salt

¾ cup olive oil

Place fennel, salad greens, chives and onion on a platter. Combine all the vinaigrette ingredients in a small bowl or jar and mix well. Season to taste. Just before serving add a small amount of dressing and toss. Add more to coat evenly.

Serves 8–10

BASIC EGG PASTA

A colorful combination of green and white pasta, called "straw and hay" by the Italians, is usually coated with a rich cheese sauce such as in our Asiago recipe. It is served as a light first course or with a meal featuring beef or veal.

*2 cups flour
   (or 1½ cups flour and ½ cup semolina)*

dash of salt

2 eggs

water as needed

Place flour and salt in a mound on table. Make a well and add eggs. With a fork, mix the flour slowly into the eggs and blend well. Add water if too dry. Gather into a ball and knead for 5–10 minutes. Cover with a bowl or place in plastic bag for 30 minutes. (Dough can also be made in a food processor.) Roll dough out by hand or use a hand crank pasta machine to cut desired shapes.

   To cook, bring a large pot of water to a full rolling boil. Add the fresh pasta and cook until it floats on the top (this will only take a few minutes). Taste test a strand—it should be cooked but still have a bite—*al dente*. Drain very well and dot with butter to prevent sticking. Serve at once with your desired sauce.

Serves 2–4

SPINACH PASTA

*1 14-ounce or 16-ounce package fresh
   spinach, blanched, drained, squeezed dry
   and chopped, or 1 10-ounce package
   uncooked frozen spinach, thawed,
   squeezed dry and chopped*

2 eggs

2 cups flour

Place spinach and eggs in a food processor and chop fine. Add flour and process until crumbly. Add water, if needed. Turn out onto a counter and knead 2–3 minutes. Form into a ball and cover for 30 minutes before rolling out.

   Cook same as Basic Egg Pasta.

Serves 2–4

TORTORELLI'S ESCAROLE SOUP
(Zuppa di Scarola)

Save the flavorful juices left over in chicken dishes and freeze. Use this in the recipe in place of the same amount of stock—the flavor will be even more intense.

1 pound sweet or mild Italian sausage

4 quarts homemade chicken stock

6 cloves garlic, minced

freshly ground pepper

*1 pound dry white beans, washed
   and drained*

*2 large heads of escarole, roughly chopped
   in ¾-inch pieces*

salt

freshly grated Romano cheese

Brown the sausage in a large soup pot. Remove and slice into rounds; set aside. Add the stock, garlic and several grindings of pepper to the soup pot. Bring to a boil, reduce heat and simmer, scraping all the browned bits from the bottom of the pan. Add the beans and cook covered 1–1½ hours. Uncover and add the sausage and escarole and cook until escarole is soft. Taste and adjust seasonings. Serve with plenty of freshly grated Romano.

Serves 10–12

STUFFED FLANK STEAK WITH MARSALA MUSHROOM SAUCE

For a variation, omit the sauce, cool overnight and slice thin. Serve for a buffet or take on a picnic.

1 large flank steak, about 1¾ pounds

5 tablespoons butter

1 cup minced onion

2 cloves garlic, chopped

¾ pound ground pork

4 ounces pancetta, chopped

½ cup spinach, blanched, squeezed dry and chopped

3 tablespoons currants

2 tablespoons fresh parsley, chopped

¼ teaspoon thyme

¼ teaspoon basil

⅔ teaspoon salt and freshly ground pepper

1 egg, slightly beaten

1 large carrot, peeled, halved, each half cut lengthwise again and then pieces cut in thirds, producing 12 julienne strips

¼ pound provolone cheese cut into ⅓-inch julienne strips

2 tablespoons olive oil

2 cups beef stock

1 cup dry Marsala

½ pound domestic mushrooms, sliced

2 tablespoons fresh lemon juice

1 ounce dry porcini mushrooms, soaked in ½ cup hot water for 15 minutes, dried off and sliced

1 tablespoon cornstarch mixed with 2 tablespoons Marsala

In a saute pan melt 2 tablespoons butter. Add just ½ cup of the onions and garlic, saute 2 minutes until soft, add spinach and continue to cook 2 minutes. In a bowl add pork, pancetta, spinach mixture, currants, parsley, thyme, basil, salt and pepper and egg. Mix thoroughly and set aside. Blanch carrot strips in boiling water 1 minute; cool.

Butterfly the steak by slicing almost in half horizontally, being sure not to cut through on one side so it can be opened like a book. Open meat out flat, salt and pepper lightly. Spread spinach and pork filling to within ½ inch of the edge. Lay horizontal rows of carrots and cheese strips, leaving 1 inch between each row. Roll up steak lengthwise very tightly and secure well with toothpicks or twine.

In a large dutch oven heat olive oil. Brown steak lightly, add additional ½ cup of onions and continue to sauté for another minute. Add stock and Marsala, bring to a boil, cover and place in a preheated 350 degree oven for 90 minutes.

While the meat is cooking, melt 3 tablespoons butter in a large saute pan, toss domestic mushrooms in lemon juice, add to pan and sauté 2 minutes. Add porcini mushrooms and continue to sauté until liquid has evaporated. Add pan juices from meat, onion and mushroom liquid and reduce in half while keeping meat warm in Dutch oven.

Season sauce to taste and add cornstarch mixture. Remove meat from pan, remove toothpicks or twine and slice. Serve with sauce.

Serves 4–6

PASTA WITH ASIAGO CHEESE SAUCE

This dish is great prepared with pasta of any width and it can be served as an entree with shrimp or scallops added.

1–1½ pounds combination fresh egg and spinach pasta

¼ pound butter

2 tablespoons flour

2 cups cream

¼ teaspoon freshly grated nutmeg

1½ cups Asiago cheese, cut in small cubes

½ cup red pepper, cut in slivers

parsley

freshly ground pepper

Melt butter in a saucepan. Add flour and cook until bubbly. Whisk in cream and nutmeg until smooth and thick. Stir in cheese and whisk until it melts.

Cook pasta until *al dente* (slightly chewy), add cheese sauce and red pepper. Adjust seasoning and garnish.

Serves 6–8

PINE NUT ALMOND TART

This tart can be made early in the day or the day before serving. It's delicious served with Amaretto-flavored whipped cream.

PASTRY

1 cup flour

6 tablespoons butter, cut in slices

2 teaspoons sugar

1 egg

FILLING

½ cup apricot preserves

8 ounces almond paste

4 ounces butter

⅓ cup sugar

¼ teaspoon almond extract

4 eggs

¼ cup flour

½ teaspoon baking powder

¾ cup pine nuts

In a food processor or with a pastry blender combine the flour, butter and sugar. Blend until flour mixture resembles cornmeal, add egg and combine well. Knead the dough lightly with the heel of the hand against a smooth surface for a few seconds to distribute the butter, and reform it into a ball. Cover with plastic and refrigerate 30 minutes. Roll out pastry and fit into a 10-inch flan pan with a removable bottom. Prick bottom and place in freezer 10 minutes. Bake in a preheated 425 degree oven for 10 minutes; cool.

In a small saucepan heat apricot preserve, strain and spread over pastry.

With a mixer, combine until smooth the almond paste, butter, sugar and almond extract. Add one egg at a time, mixing until well combined. Add flour and baking powder and beat until smooth. Pour into pastry and sprinkle with pine nuts. Bake in 425 degree oven for 10 minutes, reduce heat to 375 degrees and continue to bake 10–15 minutes until golden brown.

Serves 12

GREAT OUTDOOR COOKING

It's a grand Wisconsin summer tradition—brats, burgers, steaks and chops on the grill. With outdoor grilling even the most reluctant cook can win accolades as a backyard chef.

If part of the appeal lies in the nearly indefinable "great outdoors taste," the no mess, no fuss preparations account for the rest. But there are a few simple preparations that can further distinguish your outdoor efforts.

For those meats that often turn dry before they're done—chicken, ribs, duck—precook in the oven and put on the grill only for the final basting stage. When you're grilling steaks, brush oil on the grill to prevent the meat from sticking. And diets aside, remember that hamburgers should contain some fat to prevent them from drying out.

If you want your brats to be the ultimate in juicy tenderness, parboil them with equal amounts of beer and water, plus some thinly sliced onions, for approximately twenty to thirty minutes. Grill until evenly browned and return to the beer / onion mixture. Keep the pot right on the grill to "hold" the brats without drying them out. Try the same method for Polish sausages and natural-casing hot dogs.

To further flavor grilled dishes, try marinades. Not only are they a tasty alternative to barbecue sauce, they also tenderize meat—particularly chicken, lamb and tougher cuts of beef.

If you've mastered the basics, this might be the summer to add to your grilling repertoire. Try fish for variety, on a well-greased grill. It takes considerably less cooking time than meat, but needs additional moisture, such as an herb-seasoned butter basting, to prevent drying.

Almost any vegetable tastes great off the grill—brush them raw or parboiled with oil or herb-seasoned butter. While cooking time will depend on the level of heat, a general guideline is that they should still hold their shape and have a slight crunch.

Fresh fruits, brushed with butter, sprinkled with sugar and skewered, can also add panache to simple menus. Choose from apple rings, spiced crab apples, pineapple chunks, halved apricots, peaches, plums, unpeeled bananas, papayas and pear halves. Watch them closely; they take just minutes to cook.

For new tastes, consider some alternatives to charcoal. Tree, shrub and herb cuttings, as well as hardwood and fruitwood chips, can be used. The two most popular chips are mesquite, from the Southwest, that burns hot and clean and imparts a distinctive smoky flavor, and hickory, an aromatic wood that's cheaper and more readily available.

Use wood chips by soaking a handful in water for a few minutes, then throwing them directly on the hot coals toward the end of grilling. Herb and grapevine cuttings add interesting flavors—place them directly on the coals toward the end of cooking or intertwine fresh herbs around meat or fish. Try fennel or dill (feathery green only) with fish or pork tenderloins, thyme or rosemary with sausages or chicken, or sage with pork or lamb.

Fresh fruits and vegetables add color and flavor to a sizzling selection of meats grilled over smoky wood chips.

WISCONSIN BURGERS

For variety, use different cheeses—such as Muenster or brick—and add home-made french fries, assorted mustards and dill pickles for an informal and tasty summer meal.

2–3 large slices rye bread (crusts included)

2 tablespoons beer

*1 pound lean ground beef
(or a combination of meats)*

1 egg, beaten

3 thick slices chopped bacon (uncooked)

½ teaspoon caraway seeds

Swiss cheese, slices

sauerkraut, drained

*toasted thick-sliced rye or pumpernickel
bread*

In a large bowl, soak rye bread in beer until beer is completely absorbed. Add beef, egg, bacon and caraway and blend thoroughly. Shape into patties. Grill until almost done. Add a slice of cheese on top of each and cook until melted.

Place burgers on toasted bread and top with sauerkraut. Serve piping hot.

Serves 4

GREEN GRILLED BEEF SHISH KEBAB

These shish kebabs are wonderful served hot with salad and rice pilaf or at room temperature in pita halves, with chopped green peppers, onions and tomatoes, and Yogurt Sauce.

¾ cup olive oil

¾ cup fresh lemon juice

⅓ cup red wine vinegar

4 cloves garlic, halved

4 bay leaves

*3 teaspoons fresh oregano, chopped or
1½ teaspoons dried*

*2 teaspoons fresh basil, chopped, or
⅔ teaspoon dried*

1 teaspoon salt

⅓ teaspoon freshly ground pepper

*3 pounds sirloin trimmed and cut
into 1½-inch cubes*

In a bowl combine all ingredients, adding the meat last and stirring gently to coat well. Pour into a double plastic bag, secure well and refrigerate 4 to 6 hours or overnight.

Thread meat on skewers, brush with marinade and grill, brushing several times and turning as necessary, for about 8 to 10 minutes. Serve hot, or with Yogurt Sauce.

When stringing the meat on skewers, push close together if you want meat rare and juicy, leave space between if you want it crispy and well done.

YOGURT SAUCE

*2 small thin cucumbers, peeled, seeded
and diced*

1½ teaspoons salt

1½ cups plain yogurt

⅔ cup sour cream

2 cloves garlic, minced

1 teaspoon fresh lemon juice

1 tablespoon grated onion

1½ tablespoons fresh dillweed, chopped

Place cucumber in colander and sprinkle with salt. Let drain 30 minutes, rinse and pat dry with paper towels. Place cucumber in a large bowl and gently stir in all the remaining ingredients. Cover and refrigerate at least 1 hour.

Serves 8

LIME-MARINATED CHICKEN WITH GREEN SAUCE

This recipe, served hot or cold, is great for picnics. Add a fresh fruit salad, pasta salad, French bread and sparkling wine for a truly memorable meal.

*4 whole chicken breasts, halved, skinned
and boned*

or

1 whole chicken, cut up

MARINADE

1 cup salad oil

*1 cup fresh lime juice (include the limes
in the marinade)*

1 small chopped onion

3 scallions, chopped

2 tablespoons chopped chives

*4 tablespoons chopped fresh tarragon
or 2 teaspoons dried tarragon*

1½ teaspoons salt

1 teaspoon Tabasco

Combine all marinade ingredients and place in a plastic bag with the chicken. Marinate several hours or overnight, turning often.

Grill 30–45 minutes basting frequently. Serve with Green Sauce.

GREEN SAUCE

3 scallions, chopped

¼ cup rice wine vinegar

2 egg yolks

*1½ cups assorted fresh herbs (parsley, basil,
chives, savory, tarragon, etc.)*

1 small clove garlic

¼ pound melted butter

Combine in a blender and whirl scallions, vinegar, egg yolks, herbs and garlic. Very slowly add the melted butter and blend well. Season to taste. Refrigerate until ready to serve. Pass along with the grilled chicken.

Serves 4

GRILLED RED SNAPPER

If red snapper is unavailable, try sword-fish or other very firm fish. Brush the grill liberally with oil to prevent sticking.

½ cup salted butter

1 teaspoon dried, crushed rosemary

freshly ground pepper

2½–3 pounds red snapper fillets

lemon wedges

Melt the butter and add the rosemary and pepper. Place the fillets over very hot coals. Grill, basting frequently with the rosemary-butter. Add mesquite chips during the last 5 minutes of cooking. Grill until done, 10 minutes for each inch of thickness. Serve with remaining rose-mary-butter and lemon wedges.

Serves 4

THAI CHICKEN SATAY

Tamarind, the tart seed pod of a tropical tree (and a major ingredient in Worces-tershire sauce) can be found in Asian food markets. It's available dried, in liquid con-centrates, or in sticky blocks. If unavail-able, it can be omitted from this recipe.

1 tablespoon ground coriander

4 cloves garlic, crushed

1 teaspoon salt

2 tablespoons brown sugar

*2 teaspoons tamarind dissolved
    in 2 tablespoons hot water (optional)*

1 chopped onion

juice of 2 limes

2 tablespoons soy sauce

2 tablespoons oil

*4 whole chicken breasts, boned, skinned
    and cut in large cubes*

Peanut Sauce

Combine coriander, garlic, salt, sugar, tamarind liquid, onion, lime juice, soy sauce and oil in a large bowl. Add chicken and marinate several hours or overnight.

Put chicken on skewers (if you use wooden skewers, first soak them in water for 30 minutes). Grill 8–10 minutes or until nicely browned. Baste with mari-nade and serve with Peanut Sauce, rice noodles, a cucumber salad, hot and sour soup, beer and iced coffee.

PEANUT SAUCE

1 clove garlic, minced

1 tablespoon oil

1 cup water

*1 teaspoon dried hot red chili peppers
    soaked in 1 tablespoon water for
    30 minutes*

*2 teaspoons tamarind dissolved
    in 2 tablespoons hot water*

½ teaspoon salt

1–2 tablespoons sugar, or to taste

¼ teaspoon shrimp paste (optional)

1 cup peanut butter, smooth or crunchy

Fry garlic in oil for 1 minute. Add water, chilies, tamarind liquid, salt, sugar and shrimp paste. When the mixture starts to simmer, add the peanut butter and stir until well blended. Allow to simmer 5 minutes, stirring frequently.

Serves 4

BARBECUE RIBS

For delicious, moist ribs, cook them slowly over a medium (not hot) flame.

½ cup bourbon

⅓ cup honey

¼ cup vegetable oil

¼ cup vinegar

3 tablespoons soy sauce

2 tablespoons Worcestershire sauce

3 cloves garlic, chopped

1 onion, chopped

2 tablespoons tomato paste

2 teaspoons Dijon mustard

4 dashes hot sauce

3 pounds pork ribs, cut into 3 to 4 rib sections

In a bowl combine all the ingredients, adding the ribs last and coating well. Put into a plastic bag, secure well and refrig-erate 4 to 6 hours.

Place on a grill, brush with marinade and continue turning and brushing as necessary until the ribs are cooked—about 30 minutes.

Serves 6

ZUCCHINI & TOMATOES

Whether it's because we always plant just a few too many or are generously supplied by friends, zucchini and tomatoes are frequent items on most of our summer tables. Fortunately the abundance of both have inspired many imaginative recipe ideas.

It's easy enough to decide how to use young zucchini. They're tasty in salads or appetizers, and great sautéed alone or in combination with other vegetables in butter, garlic and herbs, with a sprinkling of Parmesan cheese. But what to do with the ones you left on the vine long enough to turn them into enormous green blimps!

If it's middle-size, wash it, open it lengthwise and scrape out the seedy pulp (which has probably turned woody), leaving the firmer area next to the peel. Fill this edible container immediately or slightly steam and stuff it with a favorite rice salad or ratatouille. Save the pulp, purée and freeze it for winter soups. Don't pass up the strange-shaped or oversized zucchini—it makes a novel centerpiece, a tureen for a cold soup or a shell for a hearty entree like a robust beef or lamb stew.

Young zucchini can be shredded and frozen in manageable quantities for breads and cakes. Be sure it is drained well and squeezed dry before using as zucchini's water content is very high.

There is nothing to make you long more for fresh garden-grown tomatoes than the long months of settling for the hothouse variety. With vine-ripened tomatoes there's no need to get fancy—they're delicious just sliced and served as a stand-alone dish. There are several herbs—freshly snipped basil, dill or tarragon—and other seasonings, though,

that will make them truly gourmet. If you love bacon, lettuce and tomato sandwiches, but have sworn off high cholesterol foods, try a simple herbed tomato sandwich, using a low fat mayonnaise.

Tomatoes, too, are wonderful stuffed. Just hollow out the tomato centers (reserving the pulp for sauces) and turn the tomatoes upside down to drain, preferably for a few hours. Fit them into oiled cupcake tins (large size) so that they stay upright and retain their shape. If you're using a cold filling, stuff the tomato just minutes before serving.

The cherry tomato is terrific for salads and appetizers. And although they seem ideal for shish kebabs, their skins are tough and they become quite watery inside when heated. Italian plum tomatoes, sometimes called pear or Roma, are sweet and meaty, and make the best sauces and purées. Use green tomatoes in relishes, chutneys and pies, or simply fry them in oil, with your favorite seasonings.

Even if you're a canning novice, you should be able to put up a variety of sauces and purées. Once you've tasted the home-prepared version, you'll have a hard time settling for store bought.

A harvest of recipes for zucchini and tomatoes, from top: emerald cauliflower salad, chicken breasts with hot tomato vinaigrette, zucchini roulade and stuffed tomato.

EMERALD CAULIFLOWER SALAD

A very simple salad to make ahead; the anchovies and capers add a unique flavor.

1 large cauliflower

½ cup olive oil

2 tablespoons red wine vinegar

¼ cup minced parsley

2 tablespoons chopped green onions or scallions

2 cloves garlic, minced

2 tablespoons minced zucchini skins

2 tablespoons minced green pepper

2–4 anchovies

1 tablespoon capers

1 dill pickle

salt and pepper

black olives

cherry tomatoes

Break cauliflower into florets. Parboil until just tender. Drain, cool and set aside. Combine oil, vinegar, parsley, scallions, garlic, zucchini skins, green pepper, anchovies, capers and pickle. Whirl in a blender until smooth. Adjust seasonings with salt and pepper. Combine dressing with cauliflower and toss. Add a few black olives and cherry tomatoes for color. Chill before serving.

Serves 4

ZUCCHINI ROULADE

An excellent brunch dish, which can be made the day before and brought back to room temperature. It may seem complicated, but it's not, just organize your steps.

1 cup milk

1 tablespoon each chopped carrot, celery and onion

2 sprigs parsley

1 bay leaf

1 sprig fresh thyme or ¼ teaspoon dried

Scald milk with above ingredients. Remove from heat and let mixture stand covered for 10 minutes. Strain flavored milk into a bowl and set aside to cool.

ROLL MIXTURE

1 pound zucchini, grated

1½ teaspoons salt

1 minced shallot or ½ tablespoon minced green onions

1½ tablespoons butter

¼ cup flour

4 egg yolks

6 egg whites

¼ teaspoon dried thyme

¼ teaspoon dried marjoram

salt and pepper

nutmeg

⅓ cup Parmesan cheese

Toss zucchini in colander with 1½ teaspoons salt and let stand 10 minutes. Rinse and squeeze out excess moisture. In a skillet sauté shallots in butter until softened. Add zucchini and sauté together for 5 minutes or until tender.

By pouring cooled flavored milk into saucepan in a stream, add ¼ cup of flavored milk to ¼ cup flour, whisking until mixture is smooth paste. Add remaining milk and bring to boil over high heat; boil for 30 seconds, whisking to keep smooth. Remove from heat and beat in 4 egg yolks, 1 at a time, beating well after each addition. Add dried thyme and marjoram and season with salt, pepper and dash of nutmeg. Combine zucchini and sauce.

Beat 6 egg whites with pinch of salt until they hold stiff peaks. Stir ¼ of egg whites into zucchini mixture and fold gently. Continue to add all egg whites. Butter 11″ × 16″ jellyroll pan; line with foil and butter again; sprinkle with flour. Pour zucchini mixture into pan and spread evenly. Bake in preheated oven at 375 degrees for 15 minutes. Turn out on tea towel; sprinkle with ⅓ cup Parmesan cheese. Spread roulade with 1 cup of Mornay sauce (recipe on page 29), and roll up lengthwise, seam side down. Serve in slices with additional sauce.

Serves 10

STUFFED TOMATOES

Serve this dish as a luncheon entree with crusty bread and marinated cucumbers or as a first course to a robust meal.

6 firm large tomatoes

1 cup each minced onion and green pepper

6 tablespoons butter

1 cup minced cooked ham

1½ teaspoons cumin seed, ground

3 cups corn

½ cup heavy cream

1 teaspoon salt

½ teaspoon sugar

pepper

⅓ cup minced parsley

additional soft butter

Cut off and discard ½-inch portion from tops of tomatoes. Scoop out pulp, chop, and put in sieve to drain. Sprinkle pulp and insides of shells lightly with sugar and salt. Invert shells on paper towels and drain for 30 minutes. In skillet, sauté onion and green pepper in butter until soft. Add ham and cumin and toss mixture over high heat for 1 minute. Add tomato pulp and cook for 4 minutes. Stir in cream, corn, salt, sugar and pepper to taste and cook covered for 3 minutes. Remove skillet cover and toss mixture over high heat for 1 minute. Sprinkle drained shells with parsley and fill with corn mixture. Dot each tomato with a little butter and arrange on lightly buttered baking pan. Bake at 350 degrees for 10 minutes or until just soft. Serve hot.

Serves 6

CHICKEN BREASTS WITH HOT TOMATO VINAIGRETTE

This is a very elegant and unique entree that takes very little last minute cooking.

2 whole chicken breasts, boned and skinned

juice of 2 lemons

4 tablespoons butter

salt and pepper

1 recipe Tomato Vinaigrette

1 recipe Shredded Sautéed Zucchini

Flatten chicken breasts by pounding between waxed paper. Marinate in lemon juice 2 hours. Remove chicken from juice and pat dry. Heat butter in skillet and sauté breasts over medium high heat for 3–4 minutes on each side. Season with salt and pepper. While chicken is sautéeing, heat previously made Tomato Vinaigrette just warm to the touch (not hot). To serve, place a portion of the Tomato Vinaigrette on plate, place chicken breast on top and cover with small portion of Shredded Zucchini or a thin slice of zucchini.

HOT TOMATO VINAIGRETTE

4 tablespoons olive oil

3 pounds ripe fresh tomatoes, skinned and seeded, reserve pulp

2 tablespoons white vinegar

2 tablespoons chopped parsley

1 tablespoon chopped fresh tarragon or ½ teaspoon dried

salt and pepper

Cook pulp over medium heat 20 minutes and cool. Whirl in a blender until smooth. In non-aluminum saucepan, over high heat, reduce tomato pulp to about 1½ cups. Cool to room temperature, mix in remaining ingredients and chill until serving time.

SHREDDED ZUCCHINI

1–1½ pounds zucchini, shredded

1 teaspoon salt

3 tablespoons butter

1 clove garlic

salt and pepper

Place zucchini in colander and add 1 teaspoon salt. Let stand for 30 minutes. Rinse and squeeze dry. Melt butter in skillet; when hot, add garlic and then zucchini. Sauté over medium high heat 4 minutes. Season.

Serves 4

ZUCCHINI ENCHILADAS

Use frozen or refrigerated corn tortillas, not the preshaped ready-to-fill variety; and for a real change from the ordinary, make your enchiladas with blue corn tortillas.

1 dozen corn tortillas

5 small (1¼ pounds) zucchini, shredded

1 cup sliced black olives

3½–4 cups shredded Cheddar cheese

1 cup sour cream

minced green chilies (optional)

TOMATO AND PEPPER SAUCE

2 tablespoons oil

1 medium onion, chopped

1 green pepper, chopped

2 cloves garlic, minced

2½ pounds peeled tomatoes, coarsely chopped

1 bay leaf

1 teaspoon each basil and sugar

½ teaspoon each oregano and cumin seed, ground

¼ teaspoon cayenne

3–4 teaspoons chili powder

Heat oil in large pan. Add onion and cook, stirring frequently until limp. Add green pepper and garlic and cook, stirring until pepper is tender (about 3 minutes). Add tomatoes, breaking and chopping with a fork. Add herbs. Bring to boil, cover pan, reduce heat, and simmer 25–30 minutes to blend flavors. Remove bay leaf.

To assemble: dip each tortilla in hot sauce for about 1 minute to soften. Then fill with about ¼–⅓ cup shredded zucchini, a few olive slices and 2–3 tablespoons cheese; roll tortilla loosely. Arrange seam side down in single layer in ungreased baking dish. Spoon remaining sauce evenly over top and sprinkle with remaining cheese. Bake uncovered in 350 degree oven for 25–30 minutes or until hot and bubbly. Serve with sour cream.

Serves 6

A five-course menu that's spicy,
aromatic and honey-sweet

GREEK PICNIC

It doesn't take any more than a bit of cheese, a few olives, a loaf of bread and a piece of roasted meat to make a simple, but tasty Greek-style picnic. But this gourmet version, complete with stuffed grape leaves and a nutty dessert, will give you a wonderful sample of the foods and cooking of Greece.

Greek cuisine is sometimes Mediterranean and sometimes Middle Eastern. On the Mediterranean side are citrus fruits, leafy vegetables, seafoods, pork and wine, and on the Middle Eastern are lentils, chick-peas, yogurt, lamb and rice.

Freshness and ripeness of ingredients are crucial to all good Greek cooking, a tradition established long ago in a country in which families often grew their own produce and raised their own livestock. Vegetables play an important role in this cuisine, and are frequently served as a main course in combination with other foods. They might be stuffed with rice, cheese, meat or other vegetables, or served raw in main course salads. Herbs, especially oregano, basil, mint, dill and rosemary, are used liberally in most dishes. Almost all foods are served at room temperature—making them perfect picnic fare.

Stuffed grape leaves, or dolmades, are served with a variety of highly seasoned fillings, as both an appetizer or a main course. Preserved in brine, the leaves are bottled and sold in supermarket specialty

sections or Greek food stores. Combining meat, grain and vegetables, they are wonderfully nutritious and flavorful.

Phyllo, the thin pastry used in many main course dishes as well as desserts, is stocked in many large supermarkets or specialty food stores. These thin sheets of dough are layered into meat, vegetable and cheese pies, feta is often the cheese of choice. Baklava, one of the more familiar Greek desserts, is made from layers of phyllo, chopped nuts and honey.

Another great Greek custom is the sharing of ouzo, the anise-flavored Greek liqueur (distilled from raisins, fennel and anise), which caps off many a traditional Greek meal and has accompanied or inspired many a toast.

A Greek picnic with a combination of subtle, savory flavors: caviar dip and pita bread, grape leaves with Byzantine stuffing, cheese pie with flaky phyllo crust, and traditional anise-flavored ouzo.

CAVIAR DIP
(Taramosalata)

Great appetizer with crusty bread, pita bread triangles, or raw vegetables.

8 slices stale white bread (crusts removed)

8 ounce jar of tarama (carp roe)

1 medium onion, finely grated

2 egg yolks

½ cup lemon juice

½ cup olive oil

Soak bread in water. Squeeze to dry. Tear in small pieces and set aside. Place tarama in blender and whirl at low speed until smooth. Add onion and egg yolks and blend. Add bread and whirl until smooth. Add lemon juice and olive oil alternately in a slow stream while whirling at medium speed. Increase speed to high and blend well. Pour into a small dish, cover with plastic wrap and chill until serving time.

Makes 3 cups

GRAPE LEAVES WITH BYZANTINE STUFFING
(Dolmades)

We serve this at cocktail parties all year long with a lemon-dipping sauce—combine sour cream, homemade mayonnaise, yogurt, lemon rind and garlic; blend well and chill.

1 large jar grape leaves, drained and rinsed

2 onions, minced

2 large cloves garlic, minced

3 tablespoons oil

1 pound lean ground beef or ground lean lamb

2 cups water

1 cup long-grain rice

8 ounces Italian tomatoes, drained and finely chopped

⅔ cup dried currants

⅔ cup pine nuts or chopped walnuts

⅓ cup port

2 tablespoons dried mint

¼ cup fresh parsley, minced

1 teaspoon cinnamon

salt and pepper

water

juice from 1 lemon

Remove grape leaves, rinse off brine, and place in a dish with cold water. Let soak at least 30 minutes. (Leaves can be frozen. Simply thaw at room temperature several hours before serving.) In skillet, sauté onions and garlic in oil until soft. Add meat and lightly brown. Add water, rice, tomatoes, currants, pine nuts and port. Simmer 20 minutes or until liquid is almost absorbed and rice is still slightly crunchy. Add mint, parsley, cinnamon, salt, and pepper. Taste and adjust.

To assemble: Place leaves, dull side up, on a counter. Cut off protruding stem. Place 1 tablespoon of filling on each leaf. Fold in sides and roll up, jelly-roll style. Line a large skillet with half of the broken grape leaves and lay rolls tightly, seam side down on bottom. Add a second layer if necessary. Cover completely with the rest of the broken leaves; place a heavy plate on top of all. Add water and lemon juice to the level of the plate. Bring to a boil, lower heat and simmer 30 minutes. Drain off liquid. Remove stuffed leaves carefully to a platter, cover with plastic wrap and chill. Serve cold or at room temperature.

Makes 50 servings

CHEESE PIE
(Tiropitta)

Tiropitta is equally good served room temperature or hot from the oven. Feta cheese is quite salty; you might wish to reduce the quantity of feta if you have to cut down your salt intake.

30 sheets of phyllo (to fit pan 7 inches by 11 inches or 9 inches by 12 inches

¾ cup butter, melted

4 eggs

2 cups (about ½ pound) feta cheese, crumbled or grated

2 cups (about 1 pound) cottage cheese, small curds

2 tablespoons milk

freshly ground pepper

Brush baking pan with melted butter. Lay 10 sheets of phyllo on the bottom of pan, brushing each sheet with melted butter as it is placed in pan. Beat eggs until thick and foamy. Add cheeses and beat well. Add 2 tablespoons of melted butter and milk. Beat again, add pepper. (This procedure can also be done in a food processor by adding all the ingredients at once and processing).

Spread half of mixture over phyllo in pan. Top with another 10 sheets of phyllo, brushing butter on each sheet. Repeat with cheese mixture and phyllo. Trim excess pastry from edges. Bake in preheated moderate oven at 350 degrees for about 1¼ hours or until a deep golden brown. Let sit 10 minutes and cut into squares or triangles and serve. Pie will cut easier when cooled.

Serves 10

BROILED SKEWERED LAMB
(Souvlaki)

Make miniature souvlaki for appetizers with a yogurt-dipping sauce. For variety, use other vegetables, such as onions, zucchini, red peppers, eggplant and mushrooms on the skewers.

1 large onion, peeled and cut into ⅛ inch thick slices and separated into rings

4 tablespoons olive oil

4 tablespoons fresh lemon juice

2 teaspoons salt

1 teaspoon dried oregano

½ teaspoon freshly ground black pepper

2 pounds lean boneless lamb (or beef) preferably from leg, trimmed of excess fat and cut into 2-inch cubes

2 large, firm ripe tomatoes cut into large wedges

2 large green peppers cut into quarters, seeded, and deribbed

2 tablespoons heavy cream

cooking skewers

In a large bowl add onion rings and sprinkle with olive oil, lemon juice, salt, oregano and pepper. Add lamb and turn pieces, coat well with mixture. Marinate at room temperature for at least 2 hours, or in the refrigerator for 4 hours, turning lamb occasionally.

Light a layer of coals in a charcoal broiler and let them burn until a white ash appears on the surface, or preheat a stove broiler to its highest setting.

Remove lamb from marinade and string cubes tightly on three or four long skewers, pressing firmly together. Thread tomato wedges and green pepper quarters alternately on separate skewer. If broiling the lamb, suspend skewers side by side across the length of a roasting pan deep enough to allow a one-inch space below the meat. Brush meat evenly on all sides with the cream. Broil four inches from heat, turning skewers occasionally, until vegetables brown richly and lamb is done to your taste. For pink lamb allow 15 minutes. Vegetables take less time, and should be cooked accordingly.

Serves 4

NUT LOGS
(Saragli)

A version of the traditional Baklava made in a log shape. This delicious dessert goes fast, so you may want to double the recipe.

6 ounces finely chopped walnuts

2 ounces finely chopped almonds

2 tablespoons sugar

½ teaspoon cinnamon

24–21 inch by 9 inch sheets of phyllo dough

½ to ¾ cup melted butter

Lemon-Honey Syrup

Combine nuts, sugar and cinnamon. For each roll, place 1 sheet of phyllo with the long side facing you on a counter or work surface. Generously brush phyllo with butter. Place a second sheet on the first. Brush well with butter. Cut a third sheet in half, crumble half of it on buttered sheets. Sprinkle with ¼ cup of the nut mixture. Fold in short sides of phyllo 1½" toward center. Brush with butter. Roll up, jelly-roll fashion, forming a nine-inch-long roll. Repeat with remaining phyllo. You should have eight rolls. Place rolls, seamside down, on a baking sheet. Score each roll into three pieces. Bake at 375 degrees for 35 to 40 minutes or until golden. Place baking sheet on wire rack. Slice rolls. Pour cooled Lemon-Honey Syrup over hot pastries.

LEMON-HONEY SYRUP
1 cup water

1½ cups sugar

½ teaspoon finely shredded lemon peel

1½ tablespoons fresh lemon juice

cinnamon stick

In pan combine all ingredients. Bring to boil, reduce heat and simmer uncovered for 10 minutes. Remove cinnamon stick. Cool.

Makes 24 pieces

AUTUMN

It takes weeks for the many faces of autumn to make their way south from Lake Superior, faces as different as the showy maple forests in the north and the burnished oak woods of the south. It's a time of raking leaves and rides in the country, of landscapes that reflect the changeable weather of the season, from leaves washed in muted rainy pastels to gaudy explosions of color during the brilliant sunny days of Indian Summer. And all around is a cornucopia of agricultural delights—apples, squash and pumpkins, nuts, wild rice, cranberries—reflecting the rich seasonal palette of autumn. For the country gourmet it's one of the finest seasons, when opportunities for special menus range from the casual tailgate party to that grand November feast, Thanksgiving, and when efforts turn to putting up for winter the surplus bounty of the harvest and the hunt.

POTATOES ARE HOT

Ah, the possibilities. Hash browns for breakfast, french fries for lunch, chips for a snack, au gratins for dinner—it's no wonder potatoes are the most common staple (the second most consumed food in the United States next to milk products) in the American diet. They work for every meal and in such variety—soups, salads, plain and in casseroles, there is no vegetable more versatile.

Besides that, they're good for you, high in potassium, vitamin C and fiber; and low in calories (just ninety for a medium potato) if you eat them *au naturel*. Potatoes have been promoted as the "meal in a peel" by the Wisconsin Potato and Vegetable Growers Association.

Russets are the largest potato crop in Wisconsin—accounting for as high as seventy percent of the state's total production of potatoes. They are buff to white in color and, long and rather fat, are often known as "bakers." They are high in starch, low in moisture, and become dry and fluffy with cooking, making them the preferred variety for baking, mashing and frying. Since the Idaho potato industry waged its intensive advertising campaign a few years ago, many people connect russets with Idaho potatoes, but the Idaho is simply one type of russet.

Other common varieties are the round reds and round whites, basically boiling or mashing types. The White Atlantic is ideal for potato chips because of its low ratio of sugar to starch. Great favorites in late spring are the small red new potatoes. High in moisture content, they're ideal for potato salads and wonderful just boiled or steamed, and tossed in butter and parsley.

Potatoes like it dark and cool, not cold (between 45 to 50 degrees Fahrenheit), and should not be stored in airtight plastic bags or containers. Stored in the refrigerator they will develop a sweet taste. Exposed to light they will turn green and taste bitter.

Peels can be a great addition to a variety of dishes in taste and texture as well as nutrition. (The majority of a potato's minerals are in the cortex, the narrow layer right below the skin of the potato.) When boiling potatoes, use only a small amount of water to reduce the amount of vitamins lost in the process.

Potatoes O'Brien, made with the versatile russet, is sure to be an autumn pleaser.

CRUNCHY POTATOES

A delicious choice for brunch with sausage and eggs, or for variety add chopped country ham and grated Swiss or cheddar cheese.

4 cups baking potatoes, peeled and sliced (approximately 4 large potatoes)

⅔ cup onions, chopped

2 teaspoons salt

½–1 teaspoon freshly ground pepper

2 teaspoons paprika

1½ teaspoons rosemary, crushed

4 tablespoons butter, melted

2 tablespoons grated Parmesan cheese

In a buttered 9″×13″ pan, scatter potatoes evenly over bottom, sprinkle on onions and season with salt, pepper, paprika and rosemary. Drizzle butter over top and bake 40–45 minutes uncovered at 350 degrees.

Remove from oven and sprinkle Parmesan cheese over surface. Broil until crisp and bubbly.

Serves 4

POTATO BISQUE

A very hearty soup, great served with fresh dark bread and cheese.

4 slices thick sliced bacon, diced

2 tablespoons butter

2 cups chopped onions

1 cup carrots, diced

1 cup celery, diced

6 medium red potatoes, peeled and diced

4 cups chicken stock

1½ teaspoons salt, or to taste

1 bay leaf

1¼ teaspoons marjoram

1 teaspoon dill seed

1 teaspoon paprika

¼ teaspoon thyme

2 cups milk

¼ cup chopped fresh parsley

salt and freshly ground pepper

In a large (5 quart) pot, sauté bacon until barely crisp and set aside. Pour off bacon grease, reserving 2 tablespoons in pot. Add butter. Over medium-high heat, sauté onions, carrots, celery and potatoes until onions are transparent. Add stock, salt, bay leaf, marjoram, dill seed, paprika and thyme. Bring to boil and simmer about 1 hour until potatoes are tender but do not fall apart. Add milk, sautéed bacon, parsley and salt and pepper to taste. Heat thoroughly, remove bay leaf and serve.

Serves 8

PEAR AND POTATO SALAD

A change from the usual mayonnaise-egg-potato salad—it's especially good with baked ham or fried chicken.

5 medium potatoes

2 large pears

¼ cup vinegar

½ cup oil

¼ teaspoon freshly ground pepper

½ teaspoon salt

1 teaspoon sugar

1 tablespoon grated onion

¼ cup minced fresh parsley

Boil unpeeled potatoes for about 25 minutes, then peel and cut into chunks. Peel, core and chop pears into chunks. Place potatoes and pears in a bowl. Mix together vinegar, oil, pepper, salt, sugar and grated onion. Pour over potatoes and pears. Toss gently, taste and adjust seasoning. Add parsley and mix. Serve at room temperature.

Serves 6

POTATOES O'BRIEN

Quick and easy to prepare, and a tasty addition to any simple steak and salad dinner or lunch.

2 tablespoons butter

3 tablespoons vegetable oil

4 russet potatoes, cubed (5 cups)

1 onion, finely chopped (⅔ cup)

1 green pepper, chopped (¾ cup)

¼ cup roasted red pepper or pimento, chopped

¼ cup minced fresh parsley

salt and freshly ground pepper to taste

few grains cayenne

freshly grated Parmesan cheese

In large heavy skillet, melt butter and shortening, add potatoes, and cook until light brown and tender but firm. Add onion and green pepper, and cook 2–3 minutes. Add red pepper, parsley, salt, pepper, and cayenne. Toss lightly. Transfer to serving dish, and sprinkle with Parmesan cheese, if desired.

Serves 4–6

SAVORY POTATO PIE

A beautiful, tasty pie that can be served as an entree, side dish, or as a great addition to any buffet or picnic.

1½ tablespoons chopped fresh savory (1½ teaspoons dried)

1½ tablespoons chopped fresh basil (1½ teaspoons dried)

2 tablespoons chopped fresh chives

1 tablespoon chopped fresh parsley

2 pounds potatoes, peeled and sliced into ⅛-inch slices (6 cups)

1 cup grated cheese

6 ounces ham, cut into ½-×4-inch slices

6 tablespoons butter

salt and freshly ground pepper

1 egg beaten with 1 teaspoon water (for glaze)

2 egg yolks

8 tablespoons heavy cream

Line 9-inch pie pan with half of pie dough. In small bowl combine herbs; set aside. Layer one third of potatoes in the pie shell, sprinkle with one third each of herbs, cheese and ham slices, and dot with one third of butter. Season with salt and pepper. Repeat this layering twice. Cover with remaining half of pastry, and form decorative edge. Make a small foil funnel. Cut a ½-inch round hole in center of pastry, and insert funnel. With pastry brush, paint crust with egg-water glaze. Bake in preheated 425-degree oven for 30 minutes, then at 350 degrees for 20–30 minutes, or until potatoes are tender. In small bowl beat egg yolks and cream and pour mixture into funnel hole in pastry, shift pie pan to distribute cream. Cook additional 5–10 minutes to set.

PASTRY

3 cups flour

1¼ teaspoons salt

3 tablespoons shortening

12 tablespoons (1½ sticks) butter, chilled

⅓–½ cup ice water

In bowl or food processor, mix flour and salt. Add shortening (with on-off turns if using food processor.) Add butter and process, or cut with pastry wire, until butter is broken into pea-size pieces. Add ice water in small amounts. Toss lightly until dry ingredients have been incorporated. Place on floured working surface, and knead with heel of hand a few times. Shape into two circles, wrap in plastic or wax paper and chill 1 hour.

Serves 8

A modern menu celebrating
the bounty of the harvest

THE TASTE
OF THANKSGIVING

There's no holiday more distinctly American than our observance of Thanksgiving Day, but it also belongs to a tradition of harvest festivals as old as human history. All over the world autumn is a time for people to reflect on their blessings and give thanks for the bounty of the harvest, a bounty that is reflected in our traditional Thanksgiving menu.

In America this tradition began in November 1621, when the Pilgrims joined with the neighboring Indians in a Thanksgiving feast to celebrate the harvest that insured Plymouth Colony's survival after its harsh first year. It became a popular holiday, celebrated on different dates by individual New England colonies in the years that followed, but it wasn't celebrated nationally until George Washington issued a presidential proclamation of Thanksgiving in 1789, in honor of the new Constitution. In 1863 President Lincoln issued a moving proclamation of Thanksgiving for the last Thursday of November during the height of the Civil War. In 1941, on the eve of another national crisis, Congress officially made the fourth Thursday in November a national holiday.

The Pilgrims shared the first Thanksgiving meal with the Indians who had taught them many of the agricultural skills needed to survive in the New World. It was a menu of native game, fruits and vegetables (deer, waterfowl, wild turkey, corn, squash, nuts, crabmeat, oysters and berries) that have been the heart of the Thanksgiving menu ever since (the customary turkey dinner is inspired by the four wild turkeys said to have been served at the Pilgrims' feast).

It's likely that turkey will always be the centerpiece of the Thanksgiving menu. Its taste and texture are such that the difference between an ordinary turkey and a terrific one are usually in the preparation and the stuffing. Our recipe for sausage stuffing will make your turkey a memorable one.

The turkey is just the beginning, of course. We've planned a sumptuous feast that includes plenty of old favorites, but in slightly new, up-dated and easy-to-prepare ways. And although the menu might be a bit different from your traditional one, the spirit and meaning of the first Thanksgiving still remain.

There's more to a Thanksgiving dinner than turkey and dressing. Dazzle family and friends with this sumptuous feast.

OYSTER BISQUE

You can vary this soup by substituting chopped clams or by combining them (3–4 ounces) with oysters.

7 tablespoons butter

⅓ cup white rice

2 cloves garlic, minced

2 large onions, minced

2 tablespoons shallots, minced

3 carrots, finely julienned

2 celery stalks, finely chopped

¼ cup flour

6 cups chicken stock

2 cups dry vermouth or dry white wine

1 bottle (8 ounces) clam juice

¼ teaspoon paprika

1 bay leaf

½ teaspoon thyme

salt and freshly ground pepper

grated rind of ½ lemon

½ teaspoon Worchestershire sauce

1 pound fresh oysters

2 egg yolks

2 cups sour cream

2 tablespoons fresh parsley, minced

Melt 5 tablespoons butter in stockpot and sauté the rice for 2 minutes. Add the garlic, onions, shallots, carrots and celery and cook stirring 4–5 minutes. Mix in the flour and cook 2 minutes. Add 2 cups stock and whisk until mixture is smooth. Add the remaining stock, vermouth, clam juice, paprika, bay leaf, thyme, salt and pepper. Mix and cook over medium heat until rice is tender, 20–30 minutes. Purée one-half of the soup and return to the pan. Add the lemon rind, Worchestershire sauce and more stock, if mixture is too thick. Be careful not to boil the soup—it will curdle. You can make this soup ahead of time up to this point.

Just before serving, sauté the fresh oysters in the remaining butter until just done and firm, about 4–5 minutes. Whisk the egg yolks and sour cream and slowly add to the soup. Heat and stir until smooth. Add the oysters and heat through. Correct seasoning and serve with minced parsley.

Serves 10–12

CRANBERRY WALDORF SALAD

A colorful salad that's not too tart or too sweet. To preserve its wonderful texture and color, combine the ingredients just minutes before serving.

1 package fresh cranberries (1 pound)

⅓ cup sugar (more if desired)

¼ cup olive oil

¼ cup corn oil

2 tablespoons cider vinegar

2 teaspoons Dijon mustard

salt and freshly ground pepper

3 tart Granny Smith apples, unpeeled

2 oranges (grate first then cut-up)

1 cup toasted hazelnuts (toast at 400 degrees for 5–10 minutes)

½ cup celery, cut in diagonal slices

lettuce leaves (optional)

Cut cranberries in half. Toss with sugar and refrigerate overnight. Make the dressing: whisk together the oils, vinegar, mustard, salt, pepper and orange rind. Taste and adjust. Place apples in a bowl and toss with the dressing. Combine with remaining ingredients and serve on individual plates lined with lettuce.

Serves 12

BRUSSEL SPROUTS WITH WALNUTS

A quick, simple and attractive vegetable dish that tastes great, too.

1½ pounds brussel sprouts, damaged leaves trimmed

¾ cup walnut halves or large pieces

4 tablespoons butter

salt and freshly ground pepper

Rinse brussel sprouts. Cut an "x" into the bottom stem of each sprout with a paring knife (cut larger ones in half) and set aside. In a large saucepan bring 2 quarts of salted water to a boil, add the sprouts and simmer about 4 minutes until the color is bright green and the sprouts still have a crunch inside.

In a large sauté pan melt the butter on medium high heat; add the sprouts and walnuts and cook 2–3 minutes. Season with salt and pepper. Serve hot.

Serves 6

CURRIED CHUTNEY SPREAD

This spread has a great combination of flavors—bacon, curry, raisins, peanuts—and the great crunch of celery.

8 ounces cream cheese, room temperature

¼ teaspoon garlic salt

¼ cup sour cream

2 teaspoons curry powder (or to taste)

2 slices bacon, cooked and crumbled

2 tablespoons minced scallions

½ cup raisins

½ cup salted peanuts

1 tablespoon chutney

celery sticks

Combine all ingredients and mix. Taste and adjust seasonings. Chill several hours or overnight. Spread on celery sticks and serve.

CRABMEAT FRITTERS

Serve these rich appetizers with additional salsa for dipping and lemon wedges for zip.

1 pound crabmeat, flaked

½ cup minced scallions

½ cup corn (canned or frozen, thawed)

1 small avocado (½ cup) peeled and cut in ¼-inch pieces

1 egg

¾ cup prepared salsa (hot or mild)

⅓ cup breadcrumbs

salt

dash of Tabasco

flour

cooking oil

Combine crabmeat, onions, corn and avocado. Mix egg and salsa. Add to crabmeat mixture. Mix in breadcrumbs and season. Form into 1½-inch balls. Place on wax paper-lined baking sheet. Cover with plastic and refrigerate overnight or freeze (don't thaw before cooking).

Dust fritters with flour. Add to hot oil (enough to float fritters in) in small batches. Cook until golden brown, 2 minutes per side (3 minutes if frozen). Drain and serve with slivered scallion garnish.

Serves 6–8

CHESTNUTS & SWEET POTATOES

The sweetness of the chestnuts and potatoes are tamed by the addition of lime.

5–6 long sweet potatoes or yams (2½–3 pounds)

⅔ cup brown sugar

6 tablespoons unsalted butter

⅓ cup lime juice, fresh

¼ teaspoon salt

3 tablespoons rum

½ cup (8) chestnuts in heavy syrup, drained and halved

2 tablespoons lime zest, julienned

Combine yams and water, just enough to cover and cook until barely tender when pierced with a knife, 20–25 minutes. Drain and cool. Peel and cut in ½-inch slices. Generously butter a 9-×13-inch pan or an oval ovenproof dish. Arrange slices, overlapping slightly. (Can be made one day ahead, covered and refrigerated.)

Combine sugar, butter, lime juice and salt in a saucepan and stir until butter melts. Simmer 1 minute. Remove and stir in rum. Arrange chestnuts over yams and pour mixture on top. Bake uncovered, in a 350 degree oven for 15 minutes or until yams are tender. Baste frequently.

Just before serving, preheat broiler. Broil until chestnuts are tender and tops of yams are browned, 1–2 minutes. Garnish with lime zest.

Serves 10

SAVORY STUFFING

A perfect stuffing for turkey and any other poultry, pork or beef.

1 pound hot Italian sausage, or other pork sausage

1 cup minced onions

2 large cloves garlic, minced

1 cup green pepper, chopped

1 cup celery, chopped

1½ cups toasted walnuts, chopped

1½ cups mushrooms, chopped

2 tablespoons lemon juice

4 hard-cooked eggs, chopped

¾ cup currants

¾ cup chopped parsley

6 cups cubed bread (oatmeal, wheat, cornbread, white or a combination)

2 cups wild rice, cooked until almost done

3 apples, cored but not peeled, cubed

1–2 tablespoons salt

1½ teaspoons freshly ground pepper

1 teaspoon thyme

1 teaspoon rosemary

broth or boiling water

In a large sauté pan, fry the sausage, break up into small pieces and remove. Add to the pan drippings the onion; continue to sauté 2 minutes. Add garlic, green pepper and celery and continue to sauté 5 minutes. Add the walnuts; toss the mushrooms in the lemon juice and add to the mixture along with the eggs, currants, parsley, bread, wild rice, apples, salt, pepper, thyme and rosemary. Mix well and add enough broth to bring dressing to desired consistency.

Stuffing for a 20-pound turkey

PUMPKIN CHEESECAKE

A delightful seasonal dessert; serve with flavored whipped cream.

CRUST

1½ cups ginger snap crumbs

6 tablespoons butter, melted

¼ cup granulated sugar

CAKE

2½ pounds cream cheese, at room temperature

1¼ cups granulated sugar

4 large eggs, lightly beaten

3 egg yolks, lightly beaten

3 tablespoons all-purpose flour

2½ teaspoons ground cinnamon

1½ teaspoons ground cloves

1½ teaspoons ground ginger

½ cup heavy cream

1 tablespoon vanilla extract

2 tablespoons rum

2 tablespoons brandy (or 4 tablespoons brandy and no rum)

1 can (16 ounces) mashed pumpkin

4 tablespoons crystalized ginger, chopped

5 ounces semi-sweet chocolate, cut into pieces

2 tablespoons butter

2 tablespoons cream

2 teaspoons vanilla

In a small bowl combine the ginger snap crumbs, melted butter and sugar. Press the crumb mixture onto the bottom and partly up the sides of a greased 10-inch springform pan. Smooth the crumb mixture along the bottom to an even thickness. Chill the crust 10 minutes or until set.

In a large mixer bowl beat together the cream cheese and sugar until well combined. Add the eggs and yolks, combine until smooth.

Add the flour, cinnamon, cloves and ginger; beat in the cream, vanilla, rum, brandy and pumpkin, beating at medium speed on an electric mixer until just mixed thoroughly. Fold in crystalized ginger and set aside.

In a small sauce pan over low heat combine the chocolate, butter and cream until just melted. Remove from heat, mix well; add vanilla. Pour chocolate mixture into prepared crust, smooth and cool. Pour pumpkin mixture on top of chocolate and smooth.

Bake cheesecake in a 425 degree preheated oven for 15 minutes. Reduce oven temperature to 275 degrees and bake an additional 60 minutes. Turn off heat and leave cake in the oven overnight to cool.

Serves 12

APPLE GOODNESS

Forget what the calendar says; it is peak apple season that truly announces the arrival of autumn. And in Wisconsin there is ample opportunity to make the harvest a great family outing. About 250 commercial orchards, many open to the public during peak picking season, grow about twenty varieties of apples, with major producers in the Gays Mills, Door County and Milwaukee areas. The most common variety is McIntosh, with Cortland, Red and Golden Delicious and Paulared as runners-up.

Wisconsin's self-sufficient pioneers of the mid-nineteenth century brought their own special apple stocks with them, including Golden Russet, which will stay crisp until spring if packed carefully in barrels, and the beautiful greenish-yellow, red-striped Duchess of Oldenburg, an apple of Russian origin. One of the most popular apples of the time originated in Wisconsin near Iola, in 1872—the Northwestern Greening.

Because apples vary in taste and texture tremendously, some varieties are better suited for specific uses than others. When apples are to be used in salads, fruit bowls, or as appetizers with sharp Wisconsin cheddar, choose varieties that have an attractive appearance, texture and flavor. Red Delicious, McIntosh, Winesap and Jonathan apples are good choices, but Golden Delicious and Cortland apples are most suitable since they tend to discolor slowly. To discourage darkening of any cut or sliced apple, sprinkle it with a little lemon juice. For baking or for making open-faced tarts, use Rome Beauty or Golden Delicious apples, which retain their shape when cooked. McIntosh is a good choice with its rich, tart taste and juicy pulp. Equally good are Wealthy, Lodi, Baldwin and Yellow Transparents.

Any variety of apple can be used, even overripe or slightly bruised specimens, to make cider. Cider is not the same as canned apple juice; the latter is filtered, pasteurized and otherwise processed. Sweet cider is unprocessed juice that is sold either clear or unfiltered, pasteurized or un-pasteurized. If un-pasteurized it will eventually ferment, becoming first hard cider—which has quite a kick—and eventually, if it keeps fermenting, apple vinegar.

A freshly-baked apple mince-meat tart brings out the best flavors of autumn.

APPLE PANDOWDY WITH MAPLE CREAM SAUCE

This old-fashioned dessert is great after some brisk outdoor activities.

1 recipe pie pastry

7 cups tart cooking apples, peeled, cut in ½-inch slices

⅓ cup maple syrup

1 tablespoon flour

1 ounce salt pork (or fresh fatback plus 1 teaspoon salt)

1 teaspoon cinnamon

¼ teaspoon freshly grated nutmeg

Place apples in 10-inch round baking dish. Toss with maple syrup, flour, cinnamon and nutmeg. Blanch salt pork in boiling water for 2 minutes; cut into ¼-inch cubes and add to apple mixture. If using fresh fatback, do not blanch.

Roll dough into 12-inch circle on lightly floured surface. Fit over apple mixture. Crimp over edges. Make several air slits in dough. Bake in preheated 450-degree oven for 15 minutes. Reduce heat to 325 degrees, and bake for additional 1 hour 15 minutes. Cut crust into 1-inch squares with sharp knife, and mix into apple mixture. Bake in 400-degree oven for 10 minutes more. Serve hot with Maple Cream Sauce.

MAPLE CREAM SAUCE

(makes 1 cup)

1½ cups heavy cream

¼ cup maple syrup

¼ cup light corn syrup

In small heavy saucepan, combine all ingredients, and cook over moderate heat stirring for 5 minutes or until thickened or reduced by one-third. Serve warm or chilled.

PIE PASTRY

1½ cups flour

¼ teaspoon salt

3 tablespoons lard

3 tablespoons butter

3 tablespoons ice water

Combine flour and salt in bowl; cut in lard and butter until mixture resembles meal. Slowly add water, tossing until mixture is thoroughly blended. Form into ball and wrap in wax paper. Chill 1 hour.

Serves 8

APPLE FRITTERS IN BEER BATTER

These tasty morsels are best served while still hot and coated with cinnamon or powdered sugar.

3 large Golden Delicious apples

3 tablespoons orange juice

3 tablespoons orange-flavored liqueur

2 tablespoons sugar

½ cup powdered sugar

1½ teaspoons cinnamon

2 large eggs, separated

¾ cup beer

1 cup flour

1 tablespoon vegetable oil plus oil for frying

⅛ teaspoon cream of tartar

⅛ teaspoon salt

Peel, core and slice apples crosswise into ½-inch thick rings and arrange them on baking sheet lined with wax paper. Sprinkle apples with orange juice, liqueur and 1 tablespoon sugar. Let stand covered for 1 hour.

In one bowl sift together powdered sugar and cinnamon and set aside. In another bowl beat 2 egg yolks and add beer. Then add flour, vegetable oil and 1 tablespoon sugar; whisk this mixture until smooth. In still another bowl beat egg whites with cream of tartar and salt until they hold stiff peaks and fold them into flour mixture gently but thoroughly. In deep fryer or in deep heavy skillet heat 1 inch of vegetable oil to 375 degrees. Dip apple rings in batter one at a time. Then fry a few at a time in oil, turning them once. Cook for 3 minutes or until they are puffed and golden and transfer with a slotted spoon to paper towel to drain. Sprinkle fritters with cinnamon-sugar mixture and arrange them in napkin-lined basket.

Makes 14 fritters

APPLE SPINACH SALAD

To bring out the unique flavors of this harvest salad, toast the walnuts on a baking sheet for 7–10 minutes at 375 degrees.

1 pound fresh spinach, trimmed, washed and dried well

2 large Red Delicious apples, cored, and diced

½ cup red onion, thinly sliced

½ cup walnuts, toasted, chopped

¼ cup currants

2 tablespoons lemon juice

1 tablespoon Dijon mustard

½ teaspoon sugar

⅓ cup olive oil

⅓ cup vegetable oil

salt and pepper

In large bowl combine spinach, diced apple, red onion, walnuts and currants. In small bowl combine lemon juice, mustard, sugar. Add olive and vegetable oil in stream and whisk dressing until well combined. Whisk in salt and pepper to taste and toss salad with dressing.

Serves 6

APPLE PANCAKE

This impressive pancake is similar to a giant popover with apples. Serve immediately and don't worry if it deflates a little.

2 large eggs

½ cup milk

1 tablespoon sugar

⅓ cup flour

¼ teaspoon salt

3 tablespoons butter

1 medium Red Delicious apple, peeled, cored, and thinly sliced

2 tablespoons sugar

¼ teaspoon cinnamon

sour cream

Beat eggs with an electric mixer at medium speed, or whisk until light and foamy. Add milk and 1 tablespoon sugar, beat about 1 minute. Blend in flour and salt, mix well. Preheat oven to 450 degrees.

Melt butter in a 10-inch oven-proof skillet. Arrange apples in a single layer in skillet and cook until slightly browned and softened, about 3 minutes. Pour batter over apples, shaking pan to distribute batter evenly. Cover and cook over burner until the underside is golden brown, about 3–4 minutes. Uncover and place in oven.

Bake until pancake begins to puff and bubble, about 5 minutes. Remove from oven and carefully invert into another 10-inch or larger pre-heated skillet; or flip pancake with long, wide spatula. Return to burner and cook over medium heat an additional 2–3 minutes. Place serving platter over skillet and invert. Combine the 2 tablespoons sugar and cinnamon and sprinkle over pancakes. Serve immediately with sour cream and browned pork sausages.

Serves 2

PORK AND APPLE PIE

Either prepare in one large deep pie dish or several individual ramekins. To save time, assemble ahead, refrigerate, bake and reheat.

1 recipe Pâte Brisee

1½ pounds boneless pork shoulder or loin cut into ½-inch cubes

2 cups onion, chopped

3 tablespoons butter

¼ pound lean bacon, chopped

¾ cup apple cider

¾ cup beef stock

¼ teaspoon thyme

freshly grated nutmeg

salt and freshly ground black pepper

2 tablespoons calvados (or apple brandy or apple jack)

2 tablespoons currants

3 large Greening apples, peeled, cored, and chopped

1 tablespoon dark brown sugar

3 tablespoons flour

1 tablespoon lemon juice

1 tablespoon nutmeg, freshly grated

2 tablespoons butter

Sprinkle pork with salt and pepper and dust with 2 tablespoons of flour, shaking off the excess. In large skillet cook onions in 3 tablespoons of butter over moderate heat, stirring until onions have softened. Transfer the onions with a slotted spoon to a bowl. Add to skillet chopped bacon and 2 tablespoons of butter; cook over moderately high heat stirring until bacon is light golden brown. Add pork and sear it over high heat for 5 minutes or until lightly browned. Add apple cider, beef stock, thyme, onions, grated nutmeg; salt and pepper to taste. Bring liquid to boil and simmer mixture covered for 1½ hours. Then simmer mixture uncovered for 30 minutes or until it is thickened and the pork is tender. Stir in calvados and currants (at this point mixture can be refrigerated overnight or for a couple days).

Transfer mixture to 12-inch, deep-dish pie plate. In bowl combine the apples, brown sugar, flour, lemon juice and freshly grated nutmeg; salt and pepper to taste. Spoon apple mixture over pork mixture; dot mixtures with 2 tablespoons butter.

Roll out dough ⅛-inch thick on floured surface. Drape it over pie plate and trim edges, leaving 1-inch overhang. Fold in overhang. Crimp edges decoratively and cut several air vents in center. Use scraps for decoration. Bake pie in middle of pre-heated 375-degree oven 1 hour and let cool on a rack.

PÂTE BRISEE

1¼ cups flour

¾ stick (6 tablespoons) cold unsalted butter, cut into bits

2 tablespoons shortening

¼ teaspoon salt

2–3 tablespoons ice water

In large bowl combine flour and salt; cut in butter and shortening until it all resembles meal. Add ice water slowly, tossing until water is incorporated. Add only as much water as mixture can absorb without becoming mushy. Form dough into ball. Knead dough lightly with heel of hand against smooth surface for a few seconds to distribute butter and shortening. Re-form into ball. Cover with plastic wrap or wax paper and chill at least 1 hour.

Serves 6

APPLE MINCEMEAT TART

Our family's traditional Thanksgiving dessert, it will make a lovely presentation at any holiday gathering.

1 recipe Rich Pastry

1 jar of prepared mincemeat

2 apples, grated but not peeled

¼ cup brandy

3 Cortland or Rome Beauty apples, peeled, cored and thinly sliced

sugar

6 ounces apricot preserves

2 tablespoons fresh lemon juice

Prepare pastry and fit into 12-inch flan ring. Chill thoroughly. Combine mincemeat, grated apple and brandy. Fill tart shell with this mixture and press down lightly. Cover with apple slices arranged in overlapping circular pattern. Sprinkle lightly with sugar. Bake at 375-degrees for 30–40 minutes or until apples are soft and beginning to brown. Remove from oven and cool.

Place apricot preserves into small sauce pan. Bring to slow simmer. Add lemon juice, cool slightly, strain over cooled apple slices. Use pastry brush for even coverage.

RICH PASTRY

1⅓ cups flour

2 tablespoons sugar

6 tablespoons butter

2 tablespoons shortening

¾ teaspoon grated lemon rind

1 egg yolk

¼ teaspoon salt

Make a well in center of flour. Add sugar, butter (not too hard or soft). Cut into small pieces. Add shortening and cut into small pieces. Add lemon rind, egg yolk and salt. Work quickly with fingertips to make firm, smooth pastry. Dough should form ball and leave the tabletop or bowl fairly clean. Chill pastry for at least 30 minutes before rolling.

Serves 10

GAME CUISINE

Until recently the only way to sample game was to be, or to befriend, a hunter, since state and federal regulations prohibited selling it directly to grocers or restaurants. But now farm-raised or imported deer, wild duck, pheasant and goose, for example, can be bought at selected butcher shops and grocery stores. While there's a difference in taste and texture between the domestic and wild varieties, game farms and preserves approximate the "wild" flavor by allowing the animals to range free for their food.

On the whole, game meat (farm-raised or wild) is leaner and tougher than the chicken, beef or pork we're used to preparing. Most game meats, particularly venison, benefit from a marinade—it not only adds flavor, but it also acts as a tenderizer.

The four most readily available varieties of game are goose, duck, pheasant and venison. During the holidays wild goose is particularly popular. It is best roasted and is well suited to stuffings, particularly those with assertive ingredients —apples, chestnuts, sausage and potatoes. An average five-to-seven pound goose, stuffed, will easily serve four people.

Wild duck, depending on size, age and variety will generally serve two people. This game's strong flavor blends well when roasted with onions, garlic, herbs, berries and hearty red wine. Take care not to overcook; duck tastes best when still slightly pink. Estimate twelve minutes per pound at 450 degrees for very rare or fifteen minutes per pound at 350 degrees for well done.

For game that's delicious, exotic and slightly expensive, try pheasant. It's the most versatile of the wild birds but it tends to be lean and dry. To minimize dryness and bring out the best flavor, wrap the whole bird or just the breast portion in bacon before roasting. Pheasant has a mild but rich flavor and is often substituted in recipes calling for cut up chicken —like casseroles, stews, creamed dishes and slow braises. An average pheasant will generously serve two people.

Venison is the most versatile of these meats. The sirloin, tenderloin, medallions and rounds are tender and can be broiled, sautéed or grilled quickly without becoming dry. The tougher cuts, shoulder, stew meat and saddle should be marinated first then braised, roasted or made into stews with additional fat added. Ground venison can be substituted in any recipe calling for ground beef, but since it tends to be dry, add additional moisture or fat.

What you should get with good game is a pleasantly wild taste. Unless the meat is old, frozen too long or improperly prepared, it should not be overpowering or "gamey."

Add exciting tastes to your autumn menu with wild game. Clockwise from left: venison stroganoff, duck breasts and roast pheasant.

STUFFED GOOSE

Baste the goose frequently during roasting and serve with traditional side dishes —a tart green salad, homemade rolls, creamed onions, cranberry conserve, brussel sprouts and a fruit cobbler.

8 pound goose

5 potatoes, partially cooked, peeled and cut in chunks

1 cup chopped onions

¼ cup parsley, minced

1 teaspoon sage

goose liver chopped (optional)

4 ounces salt pork, blanched 5 minutes and finely diced

2 apples, unpeeled and coarsely chopped

1 teaspoon marjoram

salt and pepper

giblet stock or chicken stock

SAUCE

1 tablespoon minced shallots

¼ cup red wine vinegar

1 teaspoon Worchestershire sauce

¼ cup port wine

¼ cup sugar

⅓ cup currant jelly

1½ cups degreased pan juices

1½ tablespoons fat

Combine potatoes, onion, parsley, sage, liver, salt pork, apples, marjoram in a large bowl. Bind together with stock and season. Stuff and truss goose. Prick skin all over and set on a rack. Roast at 400 degrees for 30 minutes. Turn heat down to 325 and roast until tender, usually 30 minutes per pound. Remove from oven and place stuffing in a bowl. Keep warm. Let goose rest before carving.

Meanwhile make sauce. Combine all ingredients in a pan and bring to a boil. Reduce heat and simmer 3–4 minutes. Taste. If too thin, add 1 tablespoon beurre manie (1 tablespoon butter and 1 tablespoon flour kneaded together). Slice goose and pass the sauce.

Serves 5–6

DUCK BREASTS WITH RED WINE SAUCE

Duck breasts make an elegant dinner; prepared this way the duck is very similar to beef tenderloin, tender and succulent.

2 tablespoons butter

2 tablespoons vegetable oil

2 whole duck breasts, or 4 halves skinned and boned

2 shallots, minced

3 tablespoons lemon juice

½ pound mushrooms, sliced

½ tablespoon Dijon mustard

½ cup beef stock

½ cup red wine

¼ teaspoon thyme

½ cup Madeira

½ cup port

3–4 tablespoons currant jelly or preserves

2 tablespoons cornstarch with 6 tablespoons beef stock

salt and freshly ground pepper

In a large sauté pan, fry duck breasts in butter and vegetable oil until well browned on each side, about 5 minutes (depending on size). The meat should still be pink inside. Season with salt and pepper, remove duck and keep warm. In the same pan, sauté shallots in existing oil; toss mushrooms in lemon juice; add to shallots with mustard and continue to cook for 3 minutes. Add beef stock, red wine and thyme, reduce to half, add Madeira, port and continue to reduce 3–4 minutes on high heat. Add currant jelly, incorporate well, and simmer 10 minutes. Adjust seasoning, add cornstarch to beef stock mixture and cook 1–2 minutes or until transparent. Rewarm duck in sauté pan, slice and serve sauce over duck.

Serves 4

VENISON CHILI

Make this spicy dish in double or triple batches. It's great for parties and freezes beautifully, but omit the beans until just before serving.

cooking oil

1 tablespoon chili powder

1½ pounds venison, cut in small cubes

¼ pound thick sliced bacon, minced

4 cloves garlic, minced

2 onions, chopped

2 28-ounce cans Italian tomatoes, cut-up but not drained

12 ounces beer

6 ounces tomato paste

1½ tablespoons toasted cumin seed (toast on dry skillet until they pop)

½ teaspoon oregano

salt

1 tablespoon paprika

½ teaspoon cinnamon

1 teaspoon marjoram

½ teaspoon allspice

¼ teaspoon mace

¼ teaspoon ground coriander

¼ teaspoon ground cardamon

1 bay leaf

1 tablespoon black pepper

½ ounce unsweetened chocolate

1 teaspoon honey

½ teaspoon dry mustard

2–3 tablespoons cornmeal

3 cups cooked black beans (canned or homemade)

Combine 1 tablespoon oil, chili powder and venison in a bowl. Toss, cover with plastic and refrigerate overnight.

In a large Dutch oven, heat 1 tablespoon oil and cook bacon. Remove, and set aside. Toss meat with a little flour and brown in batches. Add more oil or bacon drippings; remove and set aside. Sauté the garlic and onion 1–2 minutes. Replace meat, bacon and remaining ingredients (except cornmeal and beans) and bring to a boil. Reduce heat, cover and simmer 2–3 hours or until meat is tender. Remove cover and cook liquid down slightly. Add cornmeal to thicken and add beans. Taste and adjust.

Serve with a dollop of sour cream in each bowl and an optional sprinkling of fresh chopped jalapeño peppers. Goes great with homemade corn bread and fresh fruit salad.

Serves 8–10

VENISON KEBABS

This makes a great party dish. For variety, include chunks of green, red or yellow peppers, zucchini or new potatoes and for a smoky, unique taste add hickory or mesquite chips to your grill.

thick sliced bacon, parboiled and cut in 1-inch squares

venison (tenderloin, sirloin, shoulder or round) cut in 2-inch chunks

mushroom caps

thick onion slices

MARINADE
1 cup red wine

1 sliced carrot

8 crushed peppercorns

8 juniper berries, crushed

6 bay leaves, broken

2 tablespoons fresh parsley, minced

1 onion, chopped

¼ cup strong black coffee

½ cup oil

Combine all ingredients in a deep bowl or plastic bag and add venison. Close and refrigerate overnight; turn occasionally.

SAVORY MAYONNAISE
5 cloves garlic

½ teaspoon salt

1 tablespoon Dijon mustard

2 tablespoons lemon juice

1 tablespoon Marinade

2 egg yolks

¾ cup oil

¾ cup olive oil

Place garlic, salt, mustard, lemon juice, 1 tablespoon Marinade and egg yolks in a blender; whirl until smooth. With blender running, slowly add oils until thick. Taste and adjust seasoning. Refrigerate until serving time.

Assembly
Alternate venison, bacon squares, mushroom caps and onions on skewers. Place on hot grill. Turn frequently and test for preferred doneness. Serve with salad, noodles and Savory Mayonnaise.

Serves 4

BRAISED PHEASANT

Choose a young pheasant for roasting. Cook older birds in moist heat.

1 pheasant, about 5 pounds

2 cups dry white wine

2 cups hot water

1 medium onion stuck with cloves

2 cardamon seeds, crushed

4 slices bacon, chopped

2 medium onions, sliced thin

¼ teaspoon thyme

3–4 juniper berries, crushed

2 tablespoons cornstarch mixed with 2 tablespoons cold water

salt and freshly ground pepper

Combine 1 cup wine, water, onion stuck with cloves and cardamon, pour over pheasant placed in a bowl or place in a double plastic bag and marinate overnight.

Cut pheasant in serving pieces and set aside. Fry bacon, sauté bird in a large pan turning frequently until well browned. Add sliced onions, salt and pepper, thyme, juniper berries. Add 1 cup wine, cover and reduce heat. Simmer 30 minutes or until tender. Remove to a heated platter, strain sauce, adjust seasoning and add cornstarch mixture, heat until thick and transparent, and pour over pheasant.

Serves 4

ROAST PHEASANT

Wrapping the pheasant in bacon before roasting will help keep it tender and moist.

2 small pheasants or 1 medium-sized pheasant, plucked, singed and cleaned

1–2 whole onions

1–2 stalks of celery, chopped

1–2 sprigs of parsley

1–2 large pinches of thyme

8–14 slices of bacon

salt and freshly ground pepper

Wipe birds well with a damp cloth and sprinkle cavities with a little salt and pepper. Using first amount for one bird and second for two, add to each cavity onion, celery, parsley and thyme. Truss the birds and place on their sides in a shallow pan; lay strips of bacon across the breasts, legs and thighs. Roast at 375 degrees for 15 minutes (20 minutes for a larger bird). Turn pheasants onto other side, cover with additional bacon. Baste with pan juices and roast 15 minutes more. Place birds on their backs, baste well. Cover again with bacon and roast additional 10 minutes. Remove bacon and return to the oven and brown. Season.

Serves 2–4

VENISON STROGANOFF

The dried mushrooms are essential to the rich taste of this elegant entree.

1 pound thinly sliced fresh mushrooms

juice of ½ lemon

6 tablespoons butter

1 large onion, cut in half then thinly sliced

2 tablespoons shallots, minced

1 clove garlic, minced

½ ounce dried mushrooms soaked in ½ cup hot water

4 tablespoons Madeira

1 teaspoon Worchestershire sauce

2 tablespoons brandy

1 cup beef stock

1 pound venison (tenderloin or sirloin) cut in strips

flour

1 tablespoon oil

1½ tablespoons tomato paste

1½ teaspoons tarragon

1 cup sour cream

Toss mushrooms with lemon and set aside. Melt 4 tablespoons butter and sauté onions, shallots and garlic 2–3 minutes. Add fresh and dried mushrooms (with liquid), Madeira, Worchestershire sauce, and cook until soft. Add brandy and beef stock. Heat 30 seconds and flame. When flame dies down, remove to a bowl and set aside.

Toss venison with flour. Melt remaining butter and oil. Sauté meat until just tender, 3–5 minutes. Add reserved onion mixture, tomato paste and tarragon. Cook 2 minutes. Taste and adjust. Just before serving whisk in sour cream—heat, but do not boil.

Serves 4

SWISS SPECIALTIES

The Swiss, known the world over for their exquisitely fine chocolate and marvelous Gruyère and Emmentaler cheeses, deserve equal attention for other Swiss dishes like the subtle nutmeg-laced veal sausage *kalberwurst,* the delicate fresh vegetable soups, and lesser-known Swiss cheeses like raclette and the tangy and unique sapsago.

Swiss immigrants to Wisconsin (most from the canton of Glarus, near Austria) settled primarily in Green County, founding the town of New Glarus there in 1845, after searching from New York to St. Louis for land favorable for their dairy farming and cheesemaking. The Swiss cheesemakers of Green County were the first to introduce Limburger and Swiss cheese to the United States.

The pale gold-to-white Gruyère and Emmentaler are the best-known Swiss cheeses in this country. The pre-eminent Gruyère (most popular with gourmets) has a firm texture, few, if any, holes, and a pronounced nutty taste. Emmentaler has numerous large holes (produced by carbon dioxide released during aging), and a somewhat milder taste. Both Gruyère and Emmentaler are the principal cheeses used in fondue, and both are popular in sandwiches and innumerable other cheese dishes.

Sapsago cheese, imported from Glarus, Switzerland, is a grey-green, conical-shaped, very pungent cheese made from skimmed milk and flavored with dried or milled clover. It is served grated into soup or over hot pasta with butter. Like romano and Parmesan, sapsago is a hard cheese which may be kept for years. The versatile raclette is a mild, firm Swiss, very popular with the Swiss but little known to Americans. A traditional preparation is to place a dish of the cheese near an open fire until it softens. It is then scraped in small portions onto heated plates and eaten with boiled new potatoes, pickled onions and bread. You can easily prepare this simple and elegant dish using your oven broiler at home, although specialty cheese stores sell a variety of raclette machines for tableside use. If genuine raclette cheese is unavailable, substitute fontina, Monterey Jack, or Gruyère.

A typical Swiss dinner (served at noon) begins with soup and includes a simple entree like our *Emice de Veal,* or perhaps a vegetable tart or a souffle, served with fresh vegetables, fruit, bread and cheese. The delectable finish to any Swiss meal is chocolate, whether baked into *Schokoladentorte* or simply eaten as candy. The Swiss regard chocolate as a food staple, and not just a sweet. Wonderfully rich, smooth and fine, the distinctive taste of Swiss chocolate comes from the Swiss method of fermenting the white beans to a dark red-brown, the use of alpine milk for the milk powder, and the extraordinary length of time taken conching (kneading and pounding) the chocolate for smoothness (as much as thirty times longer than other methods). The result is the loveliest chocolate to be found.

Perfect for a cold winter's night—
fondue Neufchatel-style with
Emmentaler and Gruyere cheese
and a loaf of French bread.

GREEN BEAN SALAD
(Gruener Bohnensalat)

A wonderful salad to add to your potluck list or take on a summer picnic when green beans are so plentiful.

1½ pounds green beans, trimmed and sliced

1½ cups sliced fresh mushrooms (tossed in lemon juice to keep them light in color)

⅔ cup cubed Swiss cheese

1 small onion, thinly sliced (about ½ cup)

1 tablespoon capers

3 tablespoons vinegar (or more, to taste)

¾ cup olive oil (or combination of olive and vegetable oils)

salt and freshly ground black pepper

1 teaspoon prepared mustard

2 tablespoons fresh chopped parsley

1 teaspoon dried tarragon, or 1 tablespoon fresh tarragon

1 head romaine lettuce

pimentos (optional)

Cook beans in boiling salted water until tender but still crisp. While they are cooking make a dressing with oil, vinegar, salt, pepper, mustard and parsley. Drain beans, but do not cool. Place in large bowl. Add onions and dressing and toss. Add tarragon, and let stand at room temperature for 1 hour. Add Swiss cheese, mushrooms and capers; toss and let stand at room temperature 30 minutes. Adjust seasonings. Slice lettuce horizontally, or tear into bite-sized pieces. Line large platter or individual dishes with cut lettuce; place mixture of green beans, mushrooms and cheese on top. Sprinkle with additional capers or a teaspoon of chopped pimentos.

Serves 6–8

HOME FRIED POTATOES
(Kartoffelroesti)

A traditional Swiss potato dish. Serve with an elegant meal or a country supper.

2 pounds potatoes (preferably cooked day before)

3 tablespoons butter

2 tablespoons vegetable oil

¾ teaspoon salt

Boil potatoes in their skins for about 10 minutes, or until knife sinks about 1 inch into potato without resistance. Drain, cool, and peel potatoes with small sharp knife. Cover and refrigerate at least 4 hours. Shred potatoes on grater; toss lightly with salt. In heavy 9- to 10-inch slope-sided skillet (preferably one with a nonstick cooking surface), heat butter and oil over low moderate heat. Gradually add potatoes, spreading them evenly in pan. Cook uncovered, pressing potatoes with spatula into flat cake for about 10–15 minutes. Check color on bottom with spatula. When potato cake is crusty and dark golden brown, place plate upside down over skillet. While grasping skillet and plate together, invert them quickly. Then carefully slide potato cake, browned side up, back into skillet. (If using a pan without a nonstick surface, add more butter and oil before returning potatoes to pan.) Cook for 6–8 minutes, or until bottom side of potatoes are as evenly browned as top and edges are crisp.

For variety, use lard instead of butter to cook potatoes, and cook them with 3 slices of diced bacon and with 1 small minced onion. Do not brown onions or bacon; add them directly to potato shreds. Or sauté medium-sized onion in butter until golden, and mix it well into potatoes along with ½ cup grated Gruyère or Emmentaler cheese.

Serves 4

FONDUE NEUCHATEL STYLE

The Swiss traditionally serve fondue with a pony of kirsh followed by a cup of hot tea.

½ pound Emmentaler cheese, shredded

½ pound Gruyère cheese, shredded

3 tablespoons flour

1 clove garlic

2 cups dry white wine, such as Neuchatel, Riesling, or Chablis

2 tablespoons kirsh

freshly grated nutmeg to taste

2 loaves Italian or French bread (day old), cut in cubes with a crust on each side

Dredge cheese lightly with flour. Rub ceramic chafing dish with garlic; pour in wine; set over moderate heat. When air bubbles rise to surface, add cheese by the handful, stirring constantly with a wooden spoon until cheese melts. Add kirsh and nutmeg; stir until blended.

Bring to table and keep bubbling hot over a burner. Spear bread cubes, dunk, and swirl in fondue. If fondue should become lumpy, or if liquid separates from fat, put fondue back on stove, and stir thoroughly with a wire whisk while adding ½ teaspoon cornstarch diluted with up to ½ glass of wine. This should bring fondue back to a thick creamy consistency. Cheese that is not well-aged tends to become lumpy and forms "threads." Both can be avoided by using more Gruyère cheese than Emmentaler. If fondue becomes too thick because of continuous cooking and evaporation of liquid, it can be thinned by returning it to stove, adding some warmed wine, and stirring thoroughly.

Serves 4

VEAL STRIPS IN WHITE WINE AND CREAM SAUCE
(Emince de Veau)

An elegant and light entrée to be served on a platter with thin slices of lemon.

1½ pounds boneless veal

5 tablespoons butter

3 tablespoons vegetable oil

3 tablespoons minced shallots or the white parts of scallions, finely chopped

¼ cup brandy

1 tablespoon flour

½ teaspoon salt

¼ teaspoon white pepper

1⅓ cups dry white wine (Neuchatel or Fendant)

1 cup heavy cream

grated rind of ½ lemon

2 tablespoons minced parsley

Trim meat of all fat and gristle. Cut against the grain into strips ¼"×2"×¼". In a heavy 10- to 12-inch skillet, melt butter and vegetable oil over medium high heat. Add shallots, and cook 3 minutes, or until soft and lightly golden. Increase heat. Add half the veal to shallots; cook, stirring constantly for 2 minutes. When veal is delicately colored, transfer to bowl with slotted spoon. Drop remaining veal in skillet and cook as before. Add reserved cooked veal to skillet.

Flame with brandy. When flame has died down, sprinkle veal with flour. Remove veal strips to warm platter. All juices should remain in skillet. Raise heat to high, add wine, bring to a boil. Immediately add cream, and whisk constantly. Boil briskly for 8–10 minutes, or until sauce has reduced to about half its original volume and thickened lightly. Add lemon rind, and taste for seasoning. Return veal to skillet and turn strips until thoroughly coated. Simmer over low heat until mixture thickens, about 4–5 minutes. Sprinkle with parsley. Serve immediately.

Serves 4–6

CHOCOLATE TORTE
(Schokoladentorte)

Make this very rich cake a day ahead. Serve thin slices with a dollop of whipped cream.

½ pound dark sweet chocolate (Tobler, Bernia)

½ cup butter, at room temperature

1 cup sugar

5 eggs, separated

½ teaspoon almond extract

⅞ cup sifted flour

1 teaspoon baking powder

⅔ cup cherry preserves mixed with 1 tablespoon kirsch

Chop chocolate into small pieces. Place in top part of double boiler over boiling water. Stir in butter and sugar until they are melted and mixture is smooth. Pour mixture into large mixing bowl. Add egg yolks, one at a time, beating well after each addition. Stir in almond extract. Sift in flour with baking powder. Beat egg whites until stiff. Fold into dough.

Grease 9-inch springform pan, line it with greased wax paper, and pour dough into it. Bake in preheated moderate oven at 350 degrees for 40–45 minutes or until cake tests done. Do not over bake. Cool. Split cake horizontally, and spread with cherry preserve mixture. Pour glaze over top of cake, and spread until smooth. Chill. Add second coating.

CHOCOLATE GLAZE

½ cup heavy cream

2 teaspoons instant espresso coffee

1 tablespoon butter

½ pound dark sweet chocolate

Put cream in pan, add coffee, and bring to slow boil. Add chocolate and butter; stir until melted and smooth. Let cool briefly until spreadable. Optional: press ½ cup slivered almonds onto side of frosted cake.

Serves 12

It's more than good food, it's friendly

GOOD AND GERMAN

When the pleasant chill of autumn nights starts to give way to the sharp edge of winter, it's time for a little gemütlichkeit. This German expression explains the feeling of warmth and friendship we get from simple pleasures; namely, hearty, pleasant, rib-sticking country food, robust drink and the company of good friends. Perhaps this comes naturally to us in Wisconsin, since so many of us are of German ancestry. But even those who aren't know the enjoyment of good German cooking.

To start with there are potato pancakes, sauerbraten, schnitzels and strudels. These are all popular, but rather time-consuming dishes to prepare. On the opposite ends are *eintopf,* or "one-pots." While these dishes are not always found in standard cookbooks, they are a hearty blend of ingredients that have come to stand for German country cuisine. One-pots are similar to "stews"—thicker and more robust than a soup, but not quite a boiled dinner. They feature inexpensive cuts of meat, together with whatever vegetables are available. Root vegetables are most often used, such as turnips, parsnips, carrots, potatoes and sometimes leeks.

There are countless combinations in which substitutions are easily made, such as beef rolls, veal ragout, beef in beer, sausages and beans, just to name a few. They are great party entrees—simply assemble the ingredients, put on the stove, and join your guests for an hour or so. All that's needed to complete these meals is a crisp salad, crusty dark bread and beer. Dumplings, though, can be a wonderful addition. They are made of cold boiled potatoes, warm mashed potatoes, old bread, raw potatoes or breadcrumbs, and are quite delicate when made properly. Spätzle, a tiny dumpling (or noodle) made in many forms—small rounds, long thin strips, or short, narrow pieces—is another popular side dish. Made of flour and egg, they require a deft hand to make them light and airy.

German desserts range from the rich cream-filled cakes traditionally served on New Year's Eve, to kuchen, a sweet dough filled with fruit and covered with a rich custard, to a variety of tortes. One of the most popular is the linzertorte, which is filled with fruit preserves and nuts.

Beef rolls (rinderrouladen) and spätzle typify hearty, friendly German food.

SPÄTZLE

These tasty noodles may take a little patience the first time, but we're certain they'll soon be a family favorite.

3½ cups flour

1 teaspoon salt

dash each of ground nutmeg and paprika

4 eggs, slightly beaten

¾ cup water

Sift flour, salt, and spices into a bowl. Add eggs and water. Beat batter until thick and smooth. Let rest 15 minutes. Mound batter into large metal spoon, and cut off thin slivers of dough with sharp knife or scissors. Drop dough strips into large kettle of boiling salted water. To aid in cutting the dough, dip the knife and scissors frequently in boiling water. Cook until tender, about 5 minutes. Lift out with slotted spoon, drain and place in serving dish. Serve with a little melted butter.

Serves 6

SAVORY GERMAN CARROTS

For last minute preparation, blanch carrots ahead, cool in cold water, drain, cover and set aside for several hours. Sauté butter and sugar mixture just before serving.

1 pound carrots, peeled and julienned

2 tablespoons butter

1¼ tablespoons brown sugar

1½ tablespoons vinegar

¼ teaspoon dried dill weed
   (or 1 teaspoon fresh dill, minced)

salt and freshly ground pepper

Blanch carrots until tender-crisp, about 2 minutes in boiling water. Set aside.

In a large sauté pan over high heat melt butter and brown sugar. Bring to a boil, add vinegar and carrots. Toss until carrots are glazed and a touch of golden color appears, about 3 minutes. Add dill and season with salt and pepper to taste. Toss and serve immediately.

Serves 4

BEEF IN BEER
(Rindfleisch in Bier)

One of the most flavorful beef stews we've found. Serve it the way the Germans do with parslied dumplings, rye bread, fried apple rings and plenty of dark beer.

2 pounds rolled rump, beef brisket, or lean chuck

¼ cup flour

salt and pepper

4–6 ounces salt pork or bacon, cut up

2 onions

1½ cups dark beer

1 cup water

dash ground cloves and nutmeg

4 tablespoons vinegar

2 tablespoons brown sugar

2 tablespoons chopped parsley

1 teaspoon dried thyme

Cut meat into cubes, roll in flour. Place bacon or salt pork in Dutch oven, and fry a few minutes. Add pieces of meat and brown. Add onions and cook 2–3 minutes. Blend in beer, water, spices, vinegar, brown sugar and seasonings. Bring to boil and cook until thickened. Reduce heat, cover pan, and cook 1½–2 hours or until meat is tender. Serve with dumplings and garnish with additional parsley.

Serves 6

BEEF ROLLS
(Rinderrouladen)

Dill pickles and carrots make a unique filling for these Beef Rolls. Save the savory pan juices to serve as a sauce or thicken for a gravy.

2 pounds round steak, ½-inch thick

6–8 slices bacon, cut in small pieces

1 onion, finely chopped

3 3-inch dill pickles, sliced lengthwise in quarters

Dijon mustard

2 cups carrots, peeled and sliced lengthwise in quarters

2 cups parsnips, peeled and sliced

1 teaspoon dill weed

1 6-ounce can tomato paste

1¾ cups water

¼ cup red wine

salt and pepper

flour

cooking oil

Cut beef into pieces about 3-inches square. With meat cleaver, pound cutlets very thin. Sprinkle each with salt and pepper. Spread some Dijon mustard on one side of each square, place pickle across it, add some onions and bacon, and roll it up. Secure with string or toothpicks. Dust lightly with flour. Cover bottom of heavy large skillet or Dutch oven with oil, and brown rolls on all sides, adding more oil to prevent sticking. Add remaining ingredients, bring to a boil, reduce heat, cover, and simmer 1½–2 hours. Check occasionally for sticking and add more liquid if necessary. Serve with *spätzle*, cooked vegetables, and sauerkraut. If desired, make gravy of pan liquids.

Serves 6

VEAL ONE-POT
(Eintopf)

The rich sauce transforms this stew into truly elegant dinner fare. It's good with braised leeks, and buttered noodles with poppyseeds or spätzle.

1¾–2 pounds veal breast or shoulder, cut into 1¼-inch cubes

2 tablespoons butter

1 small onion, finely chopped

¾ cup water

10 peppercorns, crushed

6 ¼-inch strips lemon peel

1 bay leaf

½ teaspoon salt

pinch of sugar

3 tablespoons butter

½ pound mushrooms, quartered

3 leeks, cut into ¾-inch lengths

1½ cups fresh cauliflower florets

Sauce

Combine veal in Dutch oven with enough water to cover. Place over medium heat and bring to a boil. Let boil 5 minutes; drain and set aside. Melt 2 tablespoons butter in Dutch oven, add onions, and sauté 3–4 minutes. Add ¾ cup water and veal. Stir in peppercorns, lemon peel, bay leaf, salt and sugar. Bring to boil, reduce heat, and simmer covered 1 hour. Melt 3 tablespoons butter in skillet. Add mushrooms and cook 3–4 minutes; set aside. Remove lemon peel and bay leaf from Dutch oven and discard. Layer mushrooms, leeks, and cauliflower in Dutch oven. Cover and cook 15 minutes or until vegetables are tender.

SAUCE

1½ tablespoons butter

1½ tablespoons flour

2 egg yolks, lightly beaten

3 tablespoons heavy cream

1 tablespoon chopped capers

juice of ½–1 lemon

1 tablespoon chopped parsley (garnish)

capers (garnish)

About 5 minutes before vegetables are done, melt 1 tablespoon butter in skillet over medium heat. Stir in flour and cook 2 minutes. Gradually drain broth from Dutch oven into flour mixture, and stir until sauce is smooth. Combine egg yolks and cream in small bowl. Slowly stir ¼ cup sauce into egg mixture. Gradually add egg mixture to sauce, stirring constantly. Mix in capers and lemon juice. Remove from heat. Taste and adjust seasonings. Transfer veal and vegetables to serving dish. Pour sauce over top. Garnish with parsley and extra capers.

Serves 4

LINZERTORTE

Cut in thin wedges—this nutty, savory torte is very rich. It can be made ahead and stored for several days in air-tight containers.

1 cup butter

1 cup sugar

1 tablespoon grated orange peel

2 teaspoons grated lemon peel

2 egg yolks

2 cups flour

1 teaspoon baking powder

2 teaspoons cinnamon

½ teaspoon cloves

¼ teaspoon salt

1 cup ground blanched almonds or walnuts or combination

1 cup good quality raspberry or blackberry preserves

2 tablespoons kirsch

With a mixer, cream together the butter and sugar. Add grated orange peel, 1 teaspoon lemon peel and egg yolks, beat well.

In a separate bowl mix dry ingredients, except nuts. Add to creamed mixture. Stir in nuts and knead dough with your hands until well combined and smooth. Wrap and chill well.

In a small bowl combine preserves, remaining lemon rind and kirsch. Set aside. Roll two-thirds of the dough about ⅓-inch thick; use extra flour if needed and press in and up sides of a 10-inch tart pan with removable bottom. Spread preserves over dough stopping short of top of pastry. Roll out remaining dough in long strips about ½-inch wide. Carefully place strips over preserves in lattice pattern extending to the pastry edge. Press ends down flatly on pastry border to secure. Bake in a 350 degree oven for 50–60 minutes until golden. Cool and dust lightly with powdered sugar.

Serves 12–14

A slice of the good life

HOME-BAKED PIES

Is there a symbol of Wisconsin home cooking more potent than a generous wedge of steaming homemade pie with a perfect sphere of ice cream poised atop the latticed crust? What is a meal in a rural cafe, or a Sunday dinner at Grandma's without the gift of good pie?

In the early days of our country, Colonial women displayed their culinary ingenuity by stretching scarce commodities into scrumptious pies. Fillings were made of apples, pears, grapes, berries, nuts and rhubarb (once called "pie plant") or vegetables. Then came custard and cream fillings which led to the creation of the humble pumpkin pie. An early Thanksgiving was postponed when one of the main pie ingredients, molasses, was delayed on a ship at sea. Today Thanksgiving still wouldn't be the same without pumpkin pie.

As our country grew, so did the variety of pies—New England favored pumpkin and shoofly pies; in the South it was chess and pecan pies; and the Midwest chose buttermilk and berry pies. Competition among piemakers led to local bake-offs, local fund raisers, and even pie-eating contests.

When pies were made regularly, no one worried about creating the perfect crust. Budding cooks observed and then imitated the process. Not so today—there are many cooks who have never watched experienced hands and they swear their crusts never turn out.

There are countless never-fail pie crust recipes. Almost any will do; the trick is how you handle the pastry. Work quickly and use a light touch when handling dough—a pastry blender or forks work best. The more you handle dough, the tougher it gets. Lard, margarine, solid shortening and butter can all be used—singly or in combination. Lard and shortening generally give the flakiest and tenderest crusts, while butter adds stability and rich flavor. Add ice cold water slowly to flour and mix completely before sprinkling on more. Roll the dough out lightly with as little flour as possible—a pastry cloth and rolling pin sleeve can be useful. Roll from the center in all directions to make a circle, rolling to the edges to avoid splitting.

If you held your breath for that part, now the fun begins. Make up a fresh berry or sliced apple filling, or whip up a custard cream pie—then sit back and enjoy being a star.

Fresh peaches in a tender, flaky crust make peach lattice pie a homemade classic.

BASIC PIE PASTRY

A basic crust, the goodness is in light handling.

2 cups all-purpose flour
¾ teaspoon salt
¾ cup shortening
6–8 tablespoons ice water

In medium-sized bowl mix flour with salt. Cut shortening into flour until pea-size lumps form. Drizzle ice water a teaspoon at a time while tossing mixture with a fork until it starts to clump together. Compact with your hands; do not knead. Or carefully use a food processor with only a few pulses. Cover and refrigerate 30 minutes. Divide dough in half. With pastry cloth and rolling pin covered with pastry stocking, roll out half the dough very thin to fit a 9-inch pie pan; trim, and refrigerate.

Makes 1 9" lattice or two 9" pies

APPLE-CURRANT PIE

Only in the Dairy State—an old Wisconsin law once required restaurants to serve apple pie with a slice of Cheddar cheese. It may no longer be on the books, but it's still a good idea especially with this flavorful rich pie.

pastry for a 2-crust 10-inch pie
5 firm apples, peeled, thinly sliced, and cored
1 tablespoon grated orange rind
⅓ cup orange juice
1 cup brown sugar
¼ teaspoon freshly grated nutmeg
1 teaspoon cinnamon
¼ teaspoon salt
½ cup flour
½ cup currants
3–4 tablespoons butter
milk or egg wash (1 egg beaten with 1 teaspoon water)

Toss sliced apples with orange rind and orange juice. Mix sugar, spices, salt, flour and currants. Add to apples. Toss gently. Place in pastry-lined 10-inch pie pan. Dot top with butter. Fit top crust on, make steam vents, and brush with milk or egg wash. Bake in a preheated 400 degree oven for 45–50 minutes or until bubbly and golden.

Serves 8

FRESH PEACH LATTICE PIE

This pie also tastes good with fresh nectarines or a combination of fruits.

2 cups unbleached all-purpose flour
¾ teaspoon salt
½ cup chilled unsalted butter
¼ cup solid vegetable shortening
1 tablespoon grated lemon peel
1 to 2 tablespoons fresh lemon juice
4 to 5 tablespoons ice water

GLAZE
⅔ cup peach jam
2 tablespoons dark rum

FILLING
½ to ¾ cup sugar (depending on sweetness of peaches)
¼ cup firmly packed brown sugar
3 tablespoons cornstarch
8 medium peaches, about 2½ pounds
2 tablespoons fresh lemon juice
½ teaspoon cinnamon
⅛ teaspoon freshly grated nutmeg
⅛ teaspoon salt
1 egg beaten with 2 teaspoons water

In large bowl combine flour and salt. Cut in butter and shortening with a pastry blender or forks until it resembles coarse meal. Sprinkle with lemon peel and toss lightly. Gradually add lemon juice and enough chilled water to make dough firm. Form into two balls and flatten. Cover with plastic and refrigerate 30 minutes.

For the Glaze combine peach jam and rum in small saucepan. Cook over medium heat until boiling; keep warm.

Make Filling in large bowl, combining sugars and cornstarch; set aside. Immerse peaches in boiling water for 2 minutes. Drain and run under cold water. Peel and cut into ½-inch slices. Place in reserved bowl with sugar mixture, toss gently to blend, sprinkle with lemon juice, cinnamon, nutmeg and salt; toss again and blend thoroughly.

Line 9- or 10-inch pie pan with dough. Brush bottom and sides of pastry with glaze, pour filling in pastry. With remaining dough and trimmings roll out and cut into strips. Arrange in lattice design atop the filling, pressing ends together; crimp decoratively. Carefully brush lattice with egg mixture. Bake 40–45 minutes in a 375 degree oven or until golden and bubbly in center. Transfer to a pie rack and let cool slightly—serve warm.

Makes a 9- or 10-inch pie

DERBY PIE

Named after the Kentucky Derby, this rich, gooey pie is similar to the traditional pecan pie with the addition of a chocolate layer.

pastry for a 9-inch bottom crust
6 tablespoons butter
1 cup brown sugar
2 tablespoons flour
3 eggs
1 cup light corn syrup
1 teaspoon vanilla
3 tablespoons bourbon
dash of salt
1 cup chocolate chips
1½ cups pecans

In a large bowl cream together butter, brown sugar and flour. Add eggs and beat mixture until smooth. Mix in corn syrup, vanilla, bourbon and salt. Spread chocolate chips in bottom of pie shell and place in preheated 350 degree oven for 3 minutes until chocolate slightly softens. Spread with a knife and cool. Spread pecans on top of chocolate, followed by filling mixture. Bake for 45 minutes or until a knife inserted halfway between center and edge comes out clean. Cool before serving.

Serves 8–10

DRUNKEN PUMPKIN PIE

A savory, full-flavored pie with nuts and rum. Serve with whipped cream for a spectacular finale.

pastry for a 10-inch bottom crust
¼ cup butter, melted
¼ cup brown sugar
¼ cup chopped walnuts or pecans
2 cups cooked puréed pumpkin
1 cup brown sugar
5 eggs, lightly beaten
½ cup dark rum
1½ cups heavy cream
2 teaspoons ground cinnamon
½ teaspoon ground ginger
½ teaspoon ground cloves
½ teaspoon ground allspice
¼ teaspoon salt
⅛ teaspoon freshly grated nutmeg

In a small bowl combine melted butter, brown sugar and walnuts. Pour mixture into prepared crust, prick crust edges with fork, and bake in preheated 425 degree oven for 5 minutes or until brown sugar mixture bubbles. Remove from oven.

In large bowl combine pumpkin, sugar, eggs, rum, cream, cinnamon, ginger, cloves, allspice, salt and nutmeg. Mix well, pour into crust, and bake in a preheated 350 degree oven for 40 minutes or until filling is firm in center.

Serves 8–10

OLD-FASHIONED BUTTERMILK PIE

This pie has a rich and refreshing lemon flavor and tastes better when made a day ahead.

pastry for a 9-inch bottom crust
½ teaspoon salt
1 teaspoon freshly grated nutmeg
2 teaspoons grated lemon rind
1½ tablespoons fresh lemon juice
1 stick unsalted butter
1½ cups sugar
3 large eggs
3 tablespoons flour
2 cups buttermilk

Combine salt, nutmeg, lemon rind, lemon juice and butter in mixer and beat until fluffy. Add sugar and beat. Add eggs one at a time. Blend in flour. Pour in buttermilk and beat well. (Mixture will appear curdled and separated, but will blend together during baking).

Turn mixture into unbaked pastry shell. Bake for 10 minutes at 450 degrees. Reduce heat to 350 degrees and bake 35 minutes or until knife inserted comes out clean. Cool before serving.

Serves 8–10

CRAZY ABOUT CRANBERRIES

Looking cheery in a loaf of bread or strung from limb to limb, cranberries say "Happy Holidays" like no other fruit we know. A traditional Thanksgiving and Christmas dinner favorite, these brilliant ruby berries make delicious sauces, breads, jams and desserts.

The cranberry's popularity goes back many centuries. Legend has it that long before European settlers came ashore to Plymouth Rock, Indians who gathered these wild berries from the marshy wetlands called them "ibimi" or "bitter berry." They used them as a dye, to calm their nerves, and even for healing since they believed cranberries had magical powers.

It was with the arrival of the Pilgrims that this fruit took its present name. The European settlers called them craneberries because they saw a likeness in the small pink blossoms to the head of a common crane. After watching the Indians' success in trading the versatile berries for goods and supplies, the Pilgrims soon turned them into a profitable business.

Wisconsin is a leading producer of cranberries, satisfying as much as a third of the nation's total demand. The cranberry harvest begins near the end of September and continues through early November. White until the weather turns cold, the berries respond to a hard frost with their characteristic ruby hues.

Today cranberries are grown in bogs —a series of well-groomed irrigated ditches that are sprayed to prevent the berries from frost damage. The bogs are flooded for harvesting, and after machines dislodge the berries from their vines, they float to the surface and are literally "corralled" by workers, and then taken to a processing plant for sorting. Unlike other fruits, cranberries are not selected by color and size, but by "bounce." The berries are bounced down a separating machine in which only the firmest pass the test.

Cranberries will keep for weeks refrigerated or for up to one year frozen. There's no need to thaw this fruit; in fact, grinding or chopping is actually easier when the berries are frozen.

We've suggested several special holiday treats that can be made well in advance, leaving plenty of time for the cook to be merry. A welcome gesture of friendship, gifts from your kitchen are even more appealing when they're presented with style. Try using inexpensive canning jars, hinged glass jars, antique Mason jars and baskets. Foods that don't require processing, like jams, jellies and marmalades, are suitable for more fragile antique containers or old-fashioned Mason jars adorned with fabrics or doilies for a festive touch.

These cranberry creations make tasteful gifts for any occasion.

CRANBERRY PECAN TASSIES

For an elegant addition to your dessert buffet, place tassies in individual paper cups.

PASTRY
6 ounces cream cheese, softened
1 cup butter, softened
2 cups flour

Blend cheese and butter. Stir in flour. Blend well and chill 1 hour. Shape into 1-inch balls. Place in ungreased miniature muffin pans, pressing dough evenly against bottom and sides.

FILLING
1 egg
¾ cup brown sugar
1 tablespoon butter, softened
1 teaspoon vanilla
½ teaspoon almond extract
dash of salt
⅓ cup fresh cranberries, finely chopped
2 tablespoons coarsely broken pecans

Beat together egg, sugar, butter, vanilla, almond extract and salt until smooth. Stir in berries and pecans. Spoon a heaping teaspoon or two into pastry cups. Bake at 325 degrees for 30–35 minutes or until filling is set. Cool in pans.

Makes 4 dozen

CRANBERRY YOGURT MUFFINS

Moist and tender muffins with a tasty combination of cranberries and coconut.

1 cup rolled oats
1 cup plain or vanilla yogurt
½ cup vegetable oil
¾ cup brown sugar
1 egg
1 cup unbleached all-purpose flour
1 teaspoon salt
½ teaspoon baking soda
1 teaspoon baking powder
1¼ cups cranberries, cut in half
¾ cup chopped walnuts
¾ cup coconut

In large bowl combine oats and yogurt, soak for 10 minutes. Add oil, sugar and egg, mix well. Sift in flour, salt, soda and baking powder. Fold in cranberries, walnuts and coconut until just blended. Spoon into greased muffin tins and bake 20 minutes in 400 degree oven.

Makes 20–24 muffins

SPICED CRANBERRY JAM

A great breakfast and brunch treat spread on hot, homemade biscuits or bread.

2 pounds cranberries
3 cups water
1 cup white vinegar
5½ cups sugar
1 teaspoon ground cinnamon
½ teaspoon ground allspice
½ teaspoon ground cloves
½ bottle liquid pectin

Bring cranberries, water (3 ounces) and vinegar to a boil and simmer 10 minutes. Add sugar and spices, mix well. Place on high heat, bring to a full rolling boil for 1 minute, stirring constantly. Remove from heat, add ½ bottle of pectin. Mix and skim off foam. Stir and skim 5 minutes to prevent floating fruit. Ladle into jelly jars and cover with paraffin.

Makes 10 half pint jars

CRANBERRY BREAD

This recipe is an adaptation from *Silver Palate's* Cranberry Bread with more fruits and nuts.

2 cups unbleached all-purpose flour
½ cup granulated sugar
1 tablespoon baking powder
½ teaspoon salt
⅔ cup fresh orange juice
2 eggs, beaten
3 tablespoons butter, melted
1 cup walnuts, coarsely chopped
1¾ cups cranberries
1 tablespoon grated orange rind

In large bowl sift together flour, sugar, baking powder and salt. Make a well in middle of sifted mixture and pour in orange juice, eggs and melted butter. Mix only until blended, do not overmix. Fold in walnuts, cranberries and orange rind.

Pour batter into greased pan and set on middle rack of oven. Bake for 45 to 50 minutes, or until toothpick inserted in center comes out clean. Remove bread from oven and cool in pan for 10 minutes before cooling completely on rack.

Makes a 9" × 4½" × 3" loaf

CRANBERRY-APPLE-PEAR SAUCE

A great accompaniment to Thanksgiving turkey, but equally good served with roast pork or chicken.

2 pounds fresh cranberries

3 apples, pared, cored, diced (½" cubes)

2 pears, pared, cored, diced (½" cubes)

1 cup golden raisins

1 cup currants

2 cups sugar

1 cup fresh orange juice

2 tablespoons grated orange peel

2 teaspoons ground cinnamon

½ teaspoon freshly grated nutmeg

1½ cups walnuts coarsely chopped

⅔ cup Cointreau or orange-flavored liqueur

In large saucepan combine all ingredients except walnuts and Cointreau and bring to a boil; reduce heat. Simmer uncovered, stirring frequently until mixture thickens, about 45 minutes. Stir in the walnuts and liqueur. Refrigerate covered 4 hours or overnight.

Serves 16–20

CRANBERRY-ORANGE CREAM TART

A beautiful tart with festive colors for the special holiday dinner. Make the filling and topping ahead of time and assemble the day to be served.

CRUST

2 cups unbleached all-purpose flour

2 tablespoons sugar

½ teaspoon salt

½ cup (1 stick) cold unsalted butter, thinly sliced

3 tablespoons cold vegetable shortening

5 tablespoons ice water

In medium bowl or food processor combine flour, sugar, and salt. Cut in butter and shortening until mixture resembles coarse crumbs. Sprinkle with 3 tablespoons ice water; toss lightly until dough begins to mass together. Gradually add additional water if necessary. Gather dough into ball and flatten into 6" disk. Wrap and refrigerate at least 1 hour.

Roll out dough on lightly-floured surface and place in 10-inch tart pan with a removable bottom. Fit bottom and sides of pan, trim excess dough, and prick bottom of crust with fork and refrigerate about 20 minutes or place in freezer for 10 minutes. Place in preheated 345 degree oven until golden, about 20 to 25 minutes. Cool on a rack.

FILLING

½ cup granulated sugar

4 egg yolks

4 tablespoons cornstarch

1½ cups milk, heated

½ vanilla bean, split lengthwise, or

1½ teaspoons vanilla extract

3 tablespoons orange liqueur

In medium bowl, beat sugar and egg yolks until thick and light colored. Whisk in cornstarch until smooth. In small saucepan, bring milk and vanilla to boil. Gradually whisk hot milk into egg mixture.

Scrape into heavy medium-sized saucepan and bring to boil over low heat and simmer, stirring for 1 minute until custard is thick and smooth. Cool to room temperature and whisk in orange liqueur.

TOPPING

2 large oranges

1 cup granulated sugar

12 ounces fresh cranberries

3 tablespoons cornstarch blended with 2 tablespoons water

½ cup chopped walnuts

Remove zest from oranges, cut into thin julienne strips. Squeeze juice from oranges. You will need 1 cup.

In small heavy saucepan simmer zest in 1 cup water until softened, about 3 minutes. Strain and return zest strips to pan. Add 1 cup cold water and sugar, bring to boil. Reduce heat and simmer, uncovered until syrup is reduced to ½ cup. With a slotted spoon, remove zest and spread strips flat on sheet of waxed paper.

Add orange juice to syrup in pan and bring to boil. Add cranberries, reduce heat and simmer, uncovered 10 minutes. Stir in cornstarch mixture and simmer, stirring until liquid thickens and clears. Cool to room temperature.

Slide baked tart shell onto a platter. Fill with pastry cream, spread evenly. Sprinkle walnuts over surface and spread cranberry mixture on top. Sprinkle candied orange zest in a border around edge. Refrigerate, covered, until ready to serve.

Serves 12

WINTER

Winter provides Wisconsinites numerous scenic, recreational and culinary delights. (Some may complain about the cold, but it's mostly for show, aimed at impressing visitors.) In reality we know winter as a showcase season—crisp, arctic nights when the stars reach down and dazzle like diamonds with wintry brilliance, bright days when the world is transformed into billowing expanses of white down. The state becomes a playground, with a host of recreational opportunities—skiing, skating, ice fishing, ice boating, snowmobiling, winter backpacking and camping. Country gourmets know winter as a time of hearty appetites, and robust menus to match. Appetizers are never more piquant, hot soups and homemade breads never more welcome, entrees never more deeply satisfying than after a winter outing. For those who preserved the surplus of the harvest, savory reminders of the growing season will last all winter long.

SAVORY SOUPS

There is probably no other culinary creation that benefits more from a great imagination than soup. Whether you're stirring up a hearty medley or a delicate purée, there is great satisfaction in artfully blending your favorite foods and flavors.

For the hearty soups, a stockpot or a large, sturdy pot of enamelware, heavy-gauge aluminum or stainless steel works best. (There are certain vegetables that react unfavorably with metal—spinach, for instance, with aluminum, and tomatoes with cast iron.) There is an inclination with soup to make large quantities "while you're at it." That works well with many soups, some actually benefit from the blending of flavors over time, but there are some ingredients that do not stand up well to aging. Green vegetables usually turn drab and shellfish turns tough.

Dense soups tend to thicken as they stand and benefit from thinning out with a bit of stock or water. Adding fresh vegetables to a leftover soup can also perk it up again. When a recipe calls for a sturdy stock, we suggest that you make it yourself or doctor up a good brand of canned stock. Bouillon cubes are a poor substitute, adding a salty and artificial taste.

Give your simmering soup a taste test from time to time. If you find it lacking, try one or two of the following ingredients to give it more zest: a thinly sliced lemon, tomato paste, minced onion, grated cheese, a pinch of curry powder—then adjust the other seasonings. Save the final salt and pepper until just before serving, as seasonings tend to concentrate while the soup reduces during simmering.

Serve your soup with style by adding attractive garnishes. They can be as simple as a frill of parsley, a pimento star, or a dollop of pesto or its French companion, rouille; or you might add crumbled bacon, slivered almonds, julienned vegetables or homemade croutons. Freeze individual servings for those times when no one has time to cook or family members are on the run. Even then, add a dash of something new to zip it up again.

Cook all soups gently, the creamy ones as well, for the ultimate texture and flavor. Use a good heavy cream if the recipe calls for it; you won't get the same quality with a substitute.

A favorite for winter—provencal soup with pesto.

CREAM OF WILD RICE SOUP

This is one of our favorite soups to serve on icy, winter nights. It's very rich, but pairs beautifully with a glass of full-bodied red wine—Burgundy or Bordeaux.

⅔ cup wild rice
½ cup onion, diced
½ cup celery, diced
½ cup carrots, diced
3–4 strips bacon, diced
2 tablespoons butter
4½ cups chicken stock
½ teaspoon thyme
1 teaspoon crushed rosemary
1½ cups heavy cream
beurre manie (1 tablespoon flour and
*   1 tablespoon butter kneaded together)*
pepper

Sauté rice, onion, celery, carrots and bacon in butter until crisp-tender, 3–4 minutes. Stir in stock and herbs. Bring to a boil, reduce heat and cover. Simmer until rice is tender, 30–40 minutes. Stir in cream. Whisk in beurre manie until soup thickens. Season. Add more stock if soup is too thick. Serve hot.

Serves 6

MILANESE VEGETABLE-BEEF SOUP

This soup is a satisfying entrée. Round out the meal with a salad, homemade grain bread and cheese.

3½–4 pound chuck roast
2 tablespoons cooking oil
2 large sweet red onions, sliced
2 carrots, thinly sliced
2 stalks celery, thinly sliced
2 cloves garlic, minced
½ cup parsley, minced
1 tablespoon salt
2 teaspoons basil, crumbled
2½ quarts water
1 can (1 pound) tomatoes, coarsely chopped
1 medium boiling potato, thinly sliced
1 9-ounce package frozen Italian green
*   beans, thawed*
2 medium zucchini, thinly sliced
2 cups fresh spinach, chopped
grated Parmesan cheese
dry red wine

Cut chuck roast in large chunks, trimming and discarding fat. Brown meat and bones in oil in large kettle. Mix in onions and cook until limp. Add carrots, celery, garlic, minced parsley, salt, basil and water. Bring to boil, cover, reduce heat and simmer 3 hours until meat is tender.

Remove meat and bones with slotted spoon. Discard bones and fat, return meat to soup. Refrigerate overnight or until chilled enough to skim fat from surface.

To this soup base add tomatoes, with their liquid, and potato. Bring to gentle boil and cook uncovered for 30 minutes until potato is done. Add beans and zucchini and cook 10 minutes longer. Stir in spinach and cook 3 minutes. Salt to taste. Pass Parmesan cheese and wine, so that guests can season to taste.

Serves 8–10

PROVENÇAL SOUP WITH PESTO

Fresh basil pesto may be substituted. Create different tastes by adding or substituting turnips, broccoli or cauliflower.

4 tablespoons olive oil
1 medium onion, chopped
2 leeks, chopped
5 cups water
2 carrots, sliced
1 cup zucchini, sliced
1 cup green beans, sliced 1 inch long
4 cups tomatoes
1 cup cooked navy beans
salt and pepper
¾ cup uncooked macaroni

Heat oil in large soup pot. Cook onions and leeks until soft and pale gold. Add water and carrots. Bring to boil, reduce heat, cover and simmer until carrots are barely tender. Add zucchini, green beans and tomatoes, and simmer 15 minutes more. Add navy beans and macaroni, and cook for about 15 minutes longer, until tender. Adjust seasonings. Garnish with dollop of pesto in each serving.

WINTER PESTO
2 cups parsley, stems removed
2–3 cloves garlic, minced
2 tablespoons dried basil
½ cup Parmesan cheese
2 tablespoons walnuts
½ cup olive oil
salt and pepper

Combine all ingredients in a blender. Whirl until smooth, add more oil if too thick. Place in small bowl for passing.

Serves 8–10

ACORN SQUASH BISQUE

A mild, creamy and elegant soup with a hint of thyme and rum. Prepare it a day early, adding cream and rum just before reheating.

2 leeks, chopped, white part only

4 tablespoons butter

1 large acorn squash

1½ cups chicken stock

1 teaspoon dried thyme

1 teaspoon rum

½ cup heavy cream

salt and pepper

Bake whole acorn squash in 325 degree oven for 45 minutes or until easily pierced with a fork. Scoop out pulp and set aside. Sweat leeks in large saucepan by covering with buttered round of waxed paper. Cook over medium heat about 20 minutes. Add pulp, stock, thyme, salt and pepper to taste. Combine and place in blender and whirl until smooth. Return to saucepan and cook over low heat 20 minutes. Add rum and cream just before serving and heat thoroughly. Taste and adjust seasonings. Serve hot.

Serves 4

CREAM OF TWO MUSHROOMS SOUP

Fresh shittakes, penoki and oyster mushrooms are now available in many specialty grocery stores. Add them, in combination with regular mushrooms, in this recipe for a soup with a unique flavor and texture.

8 medium dried Chinese mushrooms

1 cup boiling water

2 tablespoons butter

1½ cups fresh mushrooms, sliced

⅓ cup shallots, minced

1 teaspoon fresh lemon juice

1 tablespoon flour

1½ cups chicken stock

1 cup heavy cream

salt

¼ teaspoon white pepper, freshly ground

½ teaspoon fresh ginger root, finely grated

½ teaspoon lemon rind, grated

2 teaspoons fresh chives (or parsley), chopped

Place Chinese mushrooms in a bowl and pour boiling water over; soak 30 minutes. Drain and strain liquid through a paper towel; reserve soaking liquid. Remove woody stems from mushrooms, slice in strips; set aside.

Melt butter in pan. Stir in fresh mushrooms, shallots and lemon juice. Cover and cook 5 minutes over medium heat and remove from pan. Sprinkle flour in pan and stir. Add stock, soaking liquid and Chinese mushrooms. Heat to boiling, reduce heat and simmer, covered, 25 minutes. Stir in cream, salt, pepper, ginger root, lemon rind, chives and reserved fresh mushrooms. Simmer over low heat 5–10 minutes until slightly thick. Taste and adjust seasonings.

Serves 5–6

A cornucopia of Scandinavian specialties

SMORGASBORD BOUNTY

We have the Swedish to thank for originating the smorgasbord, and Scandinavians in general for perpetuating the tradition of this lavish feast throughout Wisconsin.

Traditionally, Swedish cooks began preparing for the holiday smorgasbord weeks ahead of the season: curing meats, pickling fish and vegetables, and making breads and cookies. The dishes are homey and wholesome, and are presented buffet-style, sometimes over several days.

Menus are divided into four courses, each of which is eaten separately. The first course is fish, and might include several varieties of herring, salmon, eel, cod and Swedish anchovies (larger and less salty than the Portuguese varieties), served with boiled new potatoes, bread and butter. The second course, usually served cold, consists of meats and cheeses: liver or veal loaf, pâté, Swedish potato sausage, assorted cheeses and meats, bread, butter and mustards. A mustard-glazed ham is often served as the main course, along with mashed potatoes, pickled beets, marinated cucumbers, sweet-and-sour cabbage, salads, lingonberry jam, pickles, bread and butter. Dessert is the final course, a tempting array of almond tarts, apple cakes and rich butter cookies. The table, beautifully decorated with red candles, woven table runners and apples, never seems to be empty.

Plan your smorgasbord for the holidays on a smaller scale and consider asking your guests to bring a course. A sample menu might include marinated herring, Swedish meatballs, and a few simple salads, such as pickled beets, cucumbers or red cabbage. Include brown beans and a rice porridge which is traditionally made with one almond—the lucky finder was said to have good fortune in the coming year. Place several chunks of cheese on wooden platters—perhaps Edam, Danish blue and a goat cheese like Kummelost. Add a platter of cold meats, and the traditional breads and flatbreads.

For the dessert course, a marzipan tart or an apple cake is traditional. Cap off your holiday smorgasbord with Scandivanian glogg, a hot punch made of red wine, brandy and sherry, flavored with almonds, raisins and orange peel. It is traditionally flamed for Christmas Eve celebrations.

A Christmas Eve smorgasbord (clockwise from center), with spicy Swedish meatballs, Christmas porridge, salmon marinated in dill, lingonberries, cardamon braid and limpa bread.

SALMON IN DILL
(Gravlax)

Remember to start the curing process for the gravlax 3 to 4 days ahead of serving for a true marinated flavor. Serve as part of your dinner or as an appetizer.

3 pounds fresh salmon, center cut, cleaned, and scaled

3 teaspoons white peppercorns, crushed

3 teaspoons dill

3 teaspoons coarse salt

Have fish dealer cut salmon in half lengthwise and remove the backbone and smaller bones. Place half of fish on large platter, skin-side down and sprinkle with pepper, dill and salt. Top with other half of fish, skin-side up. Envelop in plastic wrap, sealing both ends tightly. Place slightly larger platter on wrapped salmon and weight evenly—large food cans do nicely. Refrigerate, then turn fish every 12 hours, but make sure you put platter and weights back on fish. Continue process 3 days for maximum flavor or 2 days for minimum. When gravlax is finished, remove fish from its wrapping, scrape away seasoning and pat dry with paper towel. Place separated halves skin-side down on carving board and slice salmon halves thinly on diagonal, detaching each slice from skin.

Serves 8

PICKLED BEETS

A smorgasbord wouldn't be complete without this spicy, colorful dish. For the most flavor, marinate several days, and be sure to gently stir the mixture once or twice a day.

2–2½ cups cooked, sliced beets, drained and liquid reserved

1 medium onion, sliced in thin rings

10 tablespoons vinegar

3 tablespoons sugar

5 whole cloves, crushed

½ teaspoon salt

5 whole peppercorns, crushed

½ teaspoon whole allspice berries, crushed

2-inch piece cinnamon stick

1 large bay leaf

½ teaspoon prepared horseradish (optional)

Place beets and onions in jar or bowl. Place vinegar and ½ cup reserved beet liquid in saucepan. Bring to boil. Add remaining ingredients and bring back to boil. Pour over beets, mix, cover and chill 12 hours or overnight. Taste and adjust flavor adding more vinegar or sugar if necessary. Serve cold.

Serves 6–8

SWEDISH MEATBALLS
(Kottbullar)

Place lingonberries next to the meatballs for an interesting contrast of tastes.

1 cup fine, dry bread crumbs

1 pound ground round steak

½ pound ground pork

½ cup mashed potatoes

¼ cup onion, minced

1 egg, beaten

1½ teaspoons salt

¼ teaspoon freshly ground pepper

¼ teaspoon allspice

¼ teaspoon nutmeg

⅛ teaspoon cloves

⅛ teaspoon ginger

½ teaspoon brown sugar

2 tablespoons butter

2 tablespoons flour

⅔ cup beef broth

1 cup cream

salt and pepper

In large bowl lightly mix together one-half cup of bread crumbs, meats, potatoes, onion and egg; add spices and brown sugar and combine thoroughly. Shape mixture into balls about 1 inch in diameter; roll the balls lightly in the remaining crumbs and place on a heavy-duty cookie sheet or baking pan.

Bake in preheated, 375-degree oven for about 10 minutes; shake pan (to keep balls round). Continue to bake for additional 8–10 minutes until the meatballs are browned and shake the pan again. (At this point meatballs can be served or cooled and refrigerated or frozen for future use).

Deglaze cookie sheet with a little water on top of stove. Add pan drippings to small saucepan; add butter and melt; add flour and whisk until smooth; continue to cook 2 minutes. Add broth slowly and continue to whisk; add cream and whisk; simmer 4–5 minutes; add more milk if too thick and season to taste. Pour sauce over meatballs.

Serves 6

BROWN BEANS
(Bruna Bonor)

Prepare the day ahead, and bake just before serving.

1½ quarts water

2½ cups (about 1 pound) Swedish brown beans or kidney beans

¾ cup dark corn syrup

⅓ cup cider vinegar

1 teaspoon salt

Wash and sort beans; set aside. In large, heavy saucepan with tight-fitting cover, bring water to a boil. Add beans gradually to water so boiling will not stop. Reduce heat, cover and simmer 2 minutes. Remove saucepan from heat and set beans aside for 1 hour (or soak beans overnight in water to cover). Return saucepan to heat, cover and simmer about 1¾ hours, stirring once or twice, until beans are almost tender. (If necessary, add hot water to keep beans covered with liquid). In ovenproof dish, add corn syrup, vinegar, salt and drained beans and bake 45 minutes in 350-degree oven or until sauce thickens.

Serves 6

RICE PORRIDGE
(Risgrynsgrot)

According to Swedish custom the person who finds the almond in the porridge will have good luck within the next year.

1 tablespoon butter

1 cup rice

1 cup water

4 cups milk

1 stick cinnamon

1 teaspoon salt

4 tablespoons sugar

1 egg, beaten

½ cup golden raisins

grated rind of ½ lemon

1 whole blanched almond

Melt half of butter in large saucepan or double boiler; add rice and water; boil 10–15 minutes or until the water is absorbed. Add milk and cinnamon stick. Simmer 45 minutes or until the milk is almost absorbed; add salt and sugar; remove from heat and cool slightly. Stir in beaten egg, raisins, lemon rind and remaining butter. Pour into well-greased baking dish, stir almond into rice mixture, and bake in 400-degree oven, 45 minutes or until top turns golden.

Serves 6

MARZIPAN TART
(Mazarintarta)

Sprinkle these tarts with powdered sugar and serve small wedges with whipped cream and a fresh strawberry.

PASTRY
8 tablespoons (one stick) unsalted butter, softened

2 teaspoons sugar

¼ teaspoon salt

2 egg yolks

1¼ cups all-purpose flour

½ cup apricot preserve

To make pastry, cream butter and sugar by using electric mixer at medium speed or by using food processor until mixture is light and fluffy. Beat in salt and egg yolks one at a time; add flour and combine well. Press dough firmly into two balls. On lightly floured surface with heel of one hand, rapidly push down on portion of dough, pressing away from you in firm, quick motions, smear about 6-inches thick. (Repeat on remaining dough.) This blends fat and flour. Knead briefly into fairly smooth round ball. Flatten slightly, wrap in wax paper and chill for at least 30 minutes.

Preheat oven to 425 degrees. Roll out chilled pastry to make an 11- or 12-inch circle about ⅛-inch thick. Butter bottom and sides of 10-inch false-bottom tart pan. Press pastry into bottom and around sides of pan, turning the edges down and creating even edge. Prick bottom of shell with fork and chill for 30 minutes. Line shell with wax paper, fill paper with raw rice or beans, and bake in lower third of oven for 10 minutes. Carefully remove rice and paper. Bake 10 minutes more. When cool, spread with apricot preserve.

FRANGIPANE FILLING
1 8-ounce can almond paste at room temperature

8 tablespoons (one stick) unsalted butter, softened

⅓ cup sugar

¼ teaspoon almond extract

4 eggs

1 tablespoon flour

1 teaspoon lemon rind

½ teaspoon baking powder

½ cup sliced almonds

In medium-sized bowl, beat almond paste, crumbled with butter, sugar and almond extract until mixture is smooth. Beat in eggs one at a time, then add flour, lemon rind and baking powder, and continue to beat until smooth. Transfer to cooled pastry shell, smooth the top, and sprinkle with almonds. Bake in preheated oven for 10 minutes. Turn down heat to 375 degrees, and bake 15 minutes more or until filling is just set. Cool.

Serves 10

Great variety from the dairy state

CHEESE FOR EVERY TASTE

The first cheesemaker, it is said, was a traveler in the desert who, after days of carrying milk in a pouch made from a cow's stomach, found the liquid changed to curds. The story gets the basics right. Both the heat and rennet are necessary for curdling to occur. After that it gets complicated, with a host of variables yielding the tremendous variety of cheese products found in Wisconsin, which manufactures about a third of the nation's cheese.

While Cheddar is the most popular, you'll find the flavor varying greatly from one producer to another. Mild, medium and sharp serve as guidelines to flavor, but do not signify age. Normal aging time for a Cheddar varies from just a couple of months to four years.

Colby, a mellow, soft-textured Cheddar, bears the name of the Wisconsin town in which it was created. It has a high moisture content and is aged for only a month, making its keeping quality less than most Cheddars. Mixed with Monterey Jack it is called Cojack.

The oldest cheese invented in the state is brick, and was named for the inventor's method of pressing out the moisture with the weight of bricks. The curds were then molded into loaf or brick shapes. Brick has a wide range of flavors —midway between a Cheddar and a Limburger—going from mild to medium to quite strong. It is good in sandwiches, grated for cooking or just sliced for a cheese tray.

Swiss cheese refers to the many cheeses produced in Switzerland, in particular Emmenthaler and Gruyère. In Wisconsin we make our own mild, nutty, sweet version and call it Swiss. The characteristic holes develop from the carbon dioxide trapped in the cheese during the ripening and aging process. A good quality Swiss, aged or mild, should have a hint of moisture and appear shiny, with holes of uniform size. It is a good all-round cheese, and a favorite for fondues.

A relative newcomer to the Wisconsin cheese industry, Brie has become a popular after-dinner cheese. Ripened by molds and bacteria that are sprayed on the edible chalky exterior, it is wonderfully aromatic with a slightly pungent taste. When fully ripe, Brie will bulge slightly inside the rind and develop brownish edges.

Muenster, Limburger, Gouda, blue, Edam, mozzarella, provolone and gorgonzola are among the state's two hundred varieties of cheese. The list is international, and so is the state's reputation. Wisconsin cheeses are sent all over the world, totalling nine percent of the global market.

With over a hundred varieties to choose from in Wisconsin, there's a cheese to please any palate.

PEAR AND CHEESE SALAD

Tasty and crunchy, this salad is great at potlucks or with old-fashioned roast pork, potato and gravy dinners.

4 medium pears

1 tablespoon lemon juice

1 cup shredded Cheddar cheese

1 cup thinly sliced celery

⅓ cup roasted sunflower seeds

DRESSING

⅓ cup plain yogurt

¼ cup mayonnaise (preferably homemade)

1 teaspoon Dijon mustard

½ teaspoon grated lemon rind

⅛ teaspoon ground allspice

Core and dice unpeeled pears; mix with lemon juice. Add cheese, celery and half the sunflower seeds. Mix dressing ingredients together and pour over pears. Chill for 1–3 hours. To serve, drain salad, place in lettuce-lined bowl and sprinkle with remaining sunflower seeds.

Serves 6

COUNTRY CHEDDAR AND VEGETABLE SOUP

This soup will make a lovely simple dinner with a hearty bread, salad and a good bottle of wine.

2 cups water

1 cup carrots, minced

1 cup celery, minced

½ teaspoon thyme

¼ cup onion, minced

½ cup butter

¾ cup all-purpose flour

4 cups milk

4 cups chicken stock

1 pound sharp Cheddar cheese, grated

salt and freshly ground white pepper

cayenne pepper, salt and pepper to taste

¼ cup fresh parsley, minced

1 tablespoon fresh chives, minced

In a saucepan bring water to a boil, add carrots, celery, thyme and salt to taste, simmer 15 minutes. In kettle sauté onion in butter over moderate heat until softened, add flour. Whisk the roux over moderately low heat, about 5 minutes. Whisk in milk and stock, bring liquid to a simmer. Stirring, simmer mixture 10 minutes or until thickened. Remove kettle from heat and stir in Cheddar cheese, a little at a time, until melted. Add carrots and celery with cooking liquid, cayenne, salt and freshly ground white pepper to taste and heat soup over moderate heat, but do not boil. Add parsley, stir and continue to cook 2 to 3 minutes, but do not let boil. Garnish with chives.

Serves 10 to 12

BRIE WRAPPED IN PHYLLO

A lovely dessert, sprinkled with sliced almonds; or an elegant appetizer, served with grapes, figs or other fresh fruit.

7 sheets of phyllo pastry, cut in half making 14 square sheets

1 stick butter, melted

1 whole mid-size Brie, about 3 pounds

Butter a baking sheet. Lay 1 sheet of phyllo on a work surface (cover remaining with plastic wrap), brush with melted butter, continue same technique for three more sheets of phyllo. Set Brie on top of the buttered phyllo, fold edges up and around the cheese using additional butter to flatten edges if needed. Cover the top of Brie with six additional sheets of phyllo, brushing melted butter on each layer. Tuck ends of pastry under cheese. Turn and continue with four more sheets of phyllo brushed with butter, tucking edges under and securing with butter. Brush top and sides with butter. Preheat oven to 375 degrees, bake about 20 minutes until golden. If necessary, place under broiler for a minute to brown. Let stand 20 minutes before serving. Decorate center with small bouquet of fresh flowers and leaves.

Serves 15–20

SALTIMBOCCA
(Pork Rolls)

This is a variation on the traditional Italian veal dish. It can be made ahead of time and reheated, but make the sauce just before serving.

1¼–1½ pounds tied boneless pork roast (untie and cut each section into ¼-inch slices; pound thin)

½ cup onions, minced

2 small cloves garlic, minced

4 tablespoons butter

12–16 ounces mushrooms

1 teaspoon sage, rubbed

2 tablespoons dry white wine

4 ounces shredded mild brick cheese

5 ounces shredded ham

2 tablespoons flour

2½ cups half and half

½ tablespoon tomato paste

2½ tablespoons Parmesan cheese

grated rind of ½ lemon

salt and freshly ground pepper

Sauté onions and garlic in 2 tablespoons butter. Add 8 ounces minced mushrooms and cook until soft. Add sage and wine. Cook down until most of the liquid is absorbed. Remove and set aside.

Place equal portions of brick cheese, shredded ham, and onion-mushroom mixture over each pork slice. Roll up and secure with toothpicks. Place on oiled baking sheet and place in oven at 375 degrees. Cook until tender for 25 minutes. Remove toothpicks.

Pour liquid from baking sheet into skillet and sauté remaining mushrooms, sliced. Add flour and cook 2–3 minutes. Slowly add half and half with a wire whisk. Add tomato paste, cheese and lemon rind. Taste and adjust seasonings. Pour over pork rolls and serve.

Serves 4

SWISS ENCHILADAS

Serve these creamy flavorful enchiladas with Mexican beer and a fresh salad of tomatoes, cucumbers, jicama and red onions.

2 whole chicken breasts, poached and diced

¼ cup oil

2 large onions, thinly sliced

3 cloves garlic, chopped

1 4-ounce can green chiles, chopped

2 fresh jalapeños, seeded and chopped

1 8-ounce package cream cheese, diced

1½ cups heavy cream

2 tablespoons vinegar

¼ cup roasted red peppers, chopped

3–4 cups shredded Monterey Jack or Swiss cheese

salt and pepper

12 10-inch flour tortillas or 16 6-inch corn tortillas

GARNISH
radishes

ripe olives

coriander

avocado slices

lime wedges

cream

In a large frying pan sauté onions in 3 tablespoons oil for 5 minutes, add garlic and continue to cook over low heat, stirring occasionally until onions are limp and just beginning to brown (about 10–15 minutes). Add chiles, jalapeños, chicken, cream cheese and ¼ cup cream. Mix lightly until cheese melts. Add vinegar, peppers, salt and pepper.

In a heavy frying pan add 4 tablespoons oil, fry tortillas one at a time lightly on both sides—do not fry until firm or crisp or they will break when you roll them up. In a shallow bowl or pie plate lay the tortillas in ½ cup cream, turn until completely moistened. Spoon about ½ cup chicken filling down the center and sprinkle with cheese. Roll to enclose. Set enchiladas, seam side down, in a large baking dish, side by side. Cover evenly with ¾ cup cream. Sprinkle with remaining cheese. Bake uncovered in a 375 degree oven for 20 minutes or until hot. Garnish before serving.

Serves 6–8

DEEP FRIED CHEESE CURDS

Keep a supply of these in your freezer for a spur-of-the-moment appetizer.

1 pound cheese curds

1 bottle beer

½ cup flour

½ cup powdered milk

1½ cups buttermilk

1¼ cups finely ground bread crumbs

1 teaspoon salt

¼ teaspoon freshly ground pepper

½ teaspoon thyme

½ teaspoon oregano

1½ cups medium ground bread crumbs

vegetable oil for deep-frying

Separate the cheese curds, reserving only the medium and large size, cutting large size in half. In bowl soak curds in beer for 45 minutes to 2 hours, drain. In a shallow platter combine flour and powdered milk. Dredge drained curds in mixture, dip in buttermilk. Then dredge curds in a mixture of fine bread crumbs, half of the salt, pepper, thyme and oregano. Dip coated curds back into the buttermilk and then dredge in the mixture of the medium bread crumbs and the reserved half of the salt, pepper, thyme, and oregano. Fry in a deep fat fryer at 350 degrees for 1 to 2 minutes until golden and crisp.

Serves 8–10

WINTER PICNICS

The true initiate to life in Wisconsin has come to terms with winter—its ethereal beauty; its breathtaking cold; and most significantly, its long duration. There are, for all the days of bitter cold, many fine days when the temperature hovers between twenty and thirty-two degrees above zero, the snow crunches crisply underfoot, the trees are hung with feathery white and the air is hung with enchantment. On such days an afternoon of cross-country skiing, ice skating or a simple tramp through the woods makes the spirit and appetite soar.

On those occasions assemble a hearty winter picnic with your choice of soups, stews, meats, breads and cheeses—and forget about the calories, which you'll easily burn. Start your outdoor picnic with a rich Wisconsin Cheddar cheese soup, served with bread or crackers and fragrant meat pies. Carry the soup in a glass-lined thermos and wrap the hot meat pies in several thicknesses of foil and newspaper (these pies are also delicious cool). Pack the food in lightweight containers (plastic wear is best in cold weather) for easy carrying in your backpack.

If you have available the use of a cabin or chalet then bring along a favorite stew or our wonderful gourmet chili (which may be carried right in the cooking pot for easy reheating and serving), and complement it with our moist, Cheesy Mexican Cornbread. The chili, a favorite winter dish in Wisconsin, may be made hot or mild by varying the amounts of green and dried chilies, cayenne and jalapeños. Hot cider, hot cocoa, spicy mulled wine and hot buttered rum all suggest themselves as trailside refreshers or after-ski warmers. Be sure to include an array of raw vegetables—carrots, celery, red and green bell pepper, cauliflower, broccoli, fresh mushrooms—and cheese dip for appetizers. Finish with Skier's Chocolate Bars, our version of a portable chocolate-pecan pie.

Cheesy cornbread, spicy chili and hearty meat pies will satisfy the hungriest winter appetite.

WISCONSIN CHEDDAR CHEESE SOUP

For variety add additional vegetables such as chopped broccoli, cauliflower or turnips to this savory winter soup.

3 tablespoons butter

1 large onion, chopped

1 stalk celery, chopped

2 medium carrots, peeled and chopped

3 tablespoons flour

1¾ cups beef stock

2 medium potatoes, peeled and cubed

12 ounces dark beer (not stout or ale)

1 cup heavy cream

freshly grated nutmeg

⅛ teaspoon cayenne pepper

salt

3 cups (¾ pound) sharp Cheddar cheese, grated

In large saucepan or stockpot, sauté onion, celery and carrots in butter until soft, 4–5 minutes. Add flour and mix; cook 1 minute. Add stock slowly until well blended. Add potatoes and beer and bring to a boil. Cover, reduce heat and simmer 20 minutes or until potatoes are soft. Transfer to blender and purée. Return to pan; add cream and seasonings. Heat slowly, and add cheese in handfuls until melted. Do not boil. Adjust seasonings. Serve very hot, with garlic croutons or dark bread.

Serves 6

CHEESE DIP

This dip is great on raw vegetables and fresh tortilla chips. Just cut flour tortillas in 6 or 8 pie-shaped wedges and fry in hot oil a few seconds until golden. Drain on paper towels, salt lightly and store in an air-tight container.

1 cup sour cream

1 8-ounce package cream cheese, at room temperature

half and half

½ cup onion, finely minced

4 ounces mild green chilies, minced

Combine sour cream and cream cheese in mixer or food processor. Blend until smooth. Add enough half and half to make good dipping consistency. Stir in onions and chilies. Cover and refrigerate for several hours to blend flavors. Serve with assorted cut-up raw vegetables.

Serves 6–8

HEARTY MEAT PIES

An easy pastry even for beginners. Make sure the filling is completely cooled before assembling.

PASTRY

3 ounces cream cheese, at room temperature

8 tablespoons (1 stick) butter, no substitutes

1½ cups flour

dash of salt

Combine all ingredients in food processor and blend until ball forms by using on-off switch. Wrap in wax paper and chill 1 hour. Or place cream cheese and butter in bowl and soften. Add flour and salt, and cut in with pastry blender or fork until well blended. Form into ball, wrap in wax paper and chill 1 hour.

FILLING

1 pound beef, cut into ½-inch cubes. (Precooked pot roast or raw sirloin or pork loin cubes sautéed lightly in butter.)

4 strips slab bacon cut into small pieces

1 medium onion, chopped (about 1 cup)

1 clove garlic, chopped

2 cups mushrooms, thickly sliced

1 tablespoon fresh lemon juice

1 tablespoon butter

1 teaspoon Dijon mustard

1 cup water

1 large carrot, chopped in large chunks (about 1 cup)

¼ teaspoon dried thyme

⅛ teaspoon dried savory

3 tablespoons currants

2 tablespoons fresh parsley

1 tablespoon tomato paste

2 tablespoons red wine vinegar

½ cup fresh or frozen peas

1 teaspoon salt

¼ teaspoon freshly ground pepper

2 tablespoons flour

½ cup beef stock

In large sauté pan, cook bacon until golden brown; remove to large bowl, add beef and set aside. Pour off most of bacon fat, reserving 1 tablespoon in pan. Sauté onion and garlic in reserved fat about 3 minutes until wilted and add to cooked bacon in large bowl. Toss mushrooms with lemon juice. Melt butter in hot sauté pan and add mushrooms and mustard. Stir and cook about 3–4 minutes until most of moisture has evaporated and add to cooked bacon mixture in large bowl. Add water to pan and bring to boil; add carrot, boil 2 minutes, drain and add to bacon mixture in large bowl. Mix all ingredients well in large bowl and add thyme, savory, currants, parsley, tomato paste and vinegar. Mix well again and toss in peas, salt, pepper and flour. Add broth to ingredients in large bowl and combine well. Set aside to cool.

Divide pastry dough in half, roll out to about ⅛-inch thick. With a 6-inch inverted bowl, trace circles with a knife. Place about 3 tablespoons filling in center of each circle, pull ends up, fold over edge, and pinch ends until secure. Repeat with rest of pastry.

EGG GLAZE

1 whole egg or 1 egg yolk

2 tablespoons cream

In a small bowl mix egg yolk and cream, brush on each pie and bake in a preheated 375 degree oven about 30 minutes or until golden brown. Transfer to rack to cool.

Serves 8 to 10

MEXICAN CORN BREAD

This corn bread is so moist it can be made the day before, wrapped in foil and reheated for 10–15 minutes in a moderate 350 degree oven.

1 tablespoon corn oil
1½ cups yellow cornmeal
½ cup flour
¼ cup corn oil
1 8¾ ounce can creamed corn
2 cups (8 ounces) shredded sharp Cheddar cheese
1 cup buttermilk
2 eggs, beaten
1½ tablespoons chopped onion
⅓ cup canned green chilies, drained, seeded and chopped
2 teaspoons baking powder
1½ tablespoons sugar
1 teaspoon salt

Preheat oven to 350 degrees, grease 9- or 10-inch round or square baking pan, preferably cast iron and set aside. In large bowl, combine cornmeal, flour, corn oil, creamed corn and half of cheese and blend well. Add buttermilk, eggs, onion, chilies, baking powder, sugar and salt and mix thoroughly. Pour into prepared pan, smooth with spatula and sprinkle remaining cheese evenly over top. Bake 45 minutes to 1 hour or until done (when wooden pick inserted in center comes out clean). Crust should be lightly browned.

Serves 6–8

COUNTRY GOURMET CHILI

The chili flavor improves with age so make extra amounts for unexpected guests.

3 strips slab bacon, cut into ½-inch pieces
2 tablespoons corn oil
1¼ pounds lean pork, cut into small cubes
1 pound lean beef, cut into small cubes
3 cups onions, finely chopped
1 tablespoon garlic, finely chopped
2 green bell peppers, cored, seeded and finely chopped
1 cup celery, finely chopped
1 tablespoon dried oregano (preferably Mexican)
2 bay leaves
2 teaspoons ground cumin
1 teaspoon dried basil
3 cups plum tomatoes, chopped (including liquid if canned)
3 tablespoons tomato paste
1 bottle beer (preferably Mexican)
1½ teaspoons hot dried chilies, seeded and crushed
4 teaspoons chili powder
4 ounce can green chilies, chopped
¼ teaspoon cayenne pepper, or season to taste
2 cups cooked kidney beans, drained or one 16-ounce can kidney beans, drained
1 tablespoon pickled jalapeño pepper, finely chopped
2 teaspoons salt
¼ teaspoon freshly ground pepper
water

In large, heavy pot over medium heat, cook bacon until fat is rendered, but not crisp. Add oil, heat. Add meat in small batches and stir often until browned. Add onions, garlic, green peppers, celery, oregano, bay leaves, cumin and basil. Mix well. Add tomatoes, tomato paste, beer, dried chilies, chili powder, green chilies and cayenne. Bring the chili to boil, lower the heat and simmer 3–4 hours, stirring often. Add beans, jalapeños, salt and pepper to taste. Adjust seasoning according to taste. If desired, cook an additional 30 minutes. If too thick, add water.

Serves 6–8

SKIER'S CHOCOLATE BARS

Delightfully rich bars with layers of pastry, caramel, coconut and pecans.

1½ cups flour
⅓ cup sugar
⅛ teaspoon salt
1 small egg yolk
½ teaspoon vanilla
½ cup butter, cut into pieces
1¾ cups semisweet chocolate chips
1¼ cups shredded coconut
2 cups light brown sugar, firmly packed
2 tablespoons flour
3 eggs, beaten
1 teaspoon vanilla
1 tablespoon brandy
1½ cups pecan halves, lightly toasted

In bowl or food processor, combine flour, sugar and salt, add egg yolk, vanilla and butter and mix well (it should resemble coarse meal). With heel of your hand, work pastry on counter until well combined. Form into ball and roll out to fit 10-×12-inch baking pan. Bake in preheated 350 degree oven 15 minutes or until just beginning to turn golden. While still hot, sprinkle chocolate chips over the pastry. When chips have softened, spread evenly and sprinkle with coconut. In bowl add brown sugar, flour, eggs, vanilla and brandy. Mix well. Add pecans, pour on top of coconut and spread evenly. Bake in 350 degree oven 30 minutes until golden brown. When cool, cut into squares.

Serves 8–10

Spicy libations to cap off cold weather fun

HOT DRINKS FOR WINTER

The promise of hot toddies by the fire can make even a Wisconsin blizzard welcome. But these spicy libations are especially appealing after winter walks, late season football games, skiing, hayrides, skating—any number of cold weather activities.

Use wine, liquor, chocolate, cider, eggnog or fruit juice as the base. These recipes are simple to make and mixed in manageable quantities, unlike the pioneer recipe for "Old Madison's New Year's Punch." It's great for a "crowd," and requires forty lemons, three and one-half gallons of whiskey, one and one-half gallons brandy, two ounces whole cloves, one ounce mace, one-half ounce nutmeg, one-half ounce whole cinnamon, one gallon sherry, one gallon black currant wine, two quarts sweet grape juice and two quarts champagne!

There are several Wisconsin wines—apple, cherry, cranberry and Concord—that are ideal for warm drinks. Some are bottled spiced and just need to be gently warmed; others need to be mulled with spices and citrus peels before serving or adding to a punch.

Whatever drinks you choose, heat them slowly so they don't boil, or all the alcohol will evaporate. Keep them warm over a simmering flame, a candle warmer, an electric crockpot or coffee pot or simply in a thermos (the glass-lined types will retain temperatures longer than the plastic-lined).

For a festive presentation, serve hot drinks in heat-resistant glass or ceramic mugs or cups (metal gets too hot). Glass mugs won't crack from hot mixtures if you warm them under hot water first and place a metal teaspoon inside before pouring in the hot liquid. And for a finishing touch, include a garnish—lemon slices, cinnamon sticks, peppermint candy canes, slivered orange peels or whipped cream.

To revive drinks that have become cool, and to add a touch of showmanship, use a loggerhead. This long iron tool was used in colonial days to reheat drinks. Today you can get the same effect with a fireplace poker (just keep an extra, ash-free one on hand for these occasions), held in the fire for a few minutes and then plunged into filled mugs. The sizzle adds a great touch.

When the weather outside is frightful, there's nothing like a hot drink to warm body and soul.

HOLIDAY EGGNOG

We just slipped this one in. Although it's not a hot drink, it's a favorite for winter and holiday festivities.

6 eggs, separated
½ cup white sugar
½ cup brown sugar
1 cup bourbon
1 cup brandy
2 cups light rum
1 pint whipping cream
1 quart half and half
1 quart milk
freshly grated nutmeg

Beat egg yolks with sugar until well blended. Slowly add bourbon to yolks while continuing to beat. Add brandy and rum and mix well. Wash and dry beaters. Beat egg whites until stiff. Then beat whipping cream until stiff. Mix all ingredients in a bowl, alternating liquor mixture with egg whites, whipped cream, half and half, and milk. Chill until very cold. Stir before serving. Sprinkle with freshly grated nutmeg.

Serves 28

MEXICAN COFFEE

Great with robust coffees—French Roast, Costa Rican or New Orleans Chicory.

1 ounce Kahlua
4–6 ounces hot black coffee
ground cinnamon
sweetened whipped cream

Pour Kahlua and coffee into heatproof cups. Sprinkle lightly with cinnamon. Stir and top with whipped cream and additional cinnamon.

Serves 1

HOT TODDY

Everyone knows this is good for what ails you! Use the cinnamon stick for stirring.

1½ ounces bourbon
1 ounce ginger-flavored brandy
½ inch cinnamon stick
6 ounces apple cider or apple juice
1 teaspoon sweet butter
freshly grated nutmeg

Place the bourbon, brandy and cinnamon stick in a cup. Heat the apple cider or apple juice just to boiling. Pour over liquors. Add butter and stir until melted. Sprinkle with nutmeg. Stir again and serve.

Serves 1

BROKEN LEG OR A QUICK CURE

A very quick, hot drink. Instant relief from snow shoveling and winter's aches and pains.

1 healthy jigger bourbon
¾ cup hot apple juice or cider
seedless raisins

Put a few raisins at the bottom of a warm mug. Add the bourbon and top with hot apple juice.

Serves 1

DELUXE HOT CHOCOLATE

A chocolate-lover's hot chocolate—very rich and served plain or with flavored liqueurs.

6 ounces bittersweet or semi-sweet
*   chocolate, in pieces*
2–4 tablespoons sugar
2 cups boiling water
2 cups milk
1 cup half and half
⅔ cup Grand Marnier, Amaretto, white
*   crème de menthe, or crème de cacao*
*   (optional)*
½ cup whipping cream, whipped

Place chocolate and sugar in pan and add water. Over low heat, melt mixture and whisk frequently until smooth, 2–3 minutes. Add milk and half and half slowly. Mix well. Heat 4–6 minutes, whisking to keep smooth and prevent burning. Don't boil. Place desired liqueur in heat-proof cups and pour in hot chocolate. Mix and add a dollop of whipped cream.

Serves 4–6

CRANBERRY-ORANGE TODDY

A tart but refreshing hot drink. Float a thin orange slice on top for a festive touch.

6 cups cranberry juice cocktail
1 cup bourbon
1 teaspoon ground cinnamon
1 teaspoon freshly grated nutmeg
¾ cup orange juice
4–6 strips of orange peel, 2 inches × ½ inches
cinnamon sticks

Mix cranberry juice, bourbon, cinnamon, nutmeg, orange juice and orange peel in a large stainless steel or enamel pan. Heat just to the boiling point. Remove peel. Serve in mugs with cinnamon sticks.

Serves 6

FRIDAY'S PATROL PARKA

The perfect warm-up after a cold day of skiing or a case of sniffles and chills.

1 tablespoon honey
½ cup boiling water
½ cup warmed bourbon
1 thin slice of lemon

Combine honey and water in a warm mug. In another warm mug ignite bourbon. Pour flaming bourbon into honey and pour mixture back and forth until the flame goes out. Garnish with lemon slice.

Serves 1

HOT BUTTERED RUM

Make the batter ahead of time and refrigerate for unexpected guests.

1 stick butter, room temperature
½ cup dark brown sugar
½ teaspoon nutmeg, freshly grated
½ teaspoon ground cinnamon
¼ teaspoon ground cloves
pinch of salt
dark rum
1 ounce fresh lemon juice
hot water
lemon slices
10 cinnamon sticks (optional) for garnish

In bowl combine the butter and sugar, whisk until blended and light. Blend in nutmeg, cinnamon, cloves and salt. Pour one tablespoon of mixture, two ounces rum and one-half teaspoon lemon juice into warmed mugs and fill with hot water. Garnish with lemon slices and cinnamon sticks.

Serves 8–10

CAFE CAPPUCCINO

Preheat mugs to make this elegant after-dinner drink a real treat.

7½ ounces dark crème de cacao
5 ounces Amaretto
2½ ounces white rum
1½ ounces white crème de menthe
fresh hot coffee
whipped cream and shaved chocolate for garnish

Combine all liqueurs in a pitcher. Divide among eight preheated mugs and fill each with coffee to within one-half inch of rim. Add a dollop of whipped cream to each and top with chocolate. Serve with a straw and spoon.

Serves 8

TOM AND JERRY

Rich, creamy, hot drink that will make you mellow on the coldest of nights.

2 eggs, separated
2 tablespoons sugar
1 cup milk
1 ounce heavy cream
dash salt
¼ teaspoon ground cinnamon
⅛ teaspoon ground mace
⅛ teaspoon ground ginger
5 ounces brandy
3 ounces rum
1 pint hot milk
freshly grated nutmeg

Beat egg yolks and sugar in top of double boiler until well blended. Slowly stir in milk, cream, salt, cinnamon, mace and ginger. Cook over simmering water, stirring constantly with whisk, until mixture thickens to the consistency of a light sauce. Remove from heat. Beat egg whites until soft peaks form. Slowly stir cooked mixture into beaten egg whites. Divide among four preheated mugs. Pour 1½ ounces brandy and ¼ ounce rum into each mug. Fill mugs with hot milk. Stir. Sprinkle with nutmeg. (If egg whites are too hard and batter is too foamy, place in blender and whirl for a few seconds.)

Serves 4

SANDWICH CREATIONS

The 4th Earl of Sandwich may have made them famous, but people have been making and eating sandwiches since the Middle Ages. As the story goes, Englishmen in those days sliced bread into thick slabs which were placed directly on tables, layered with meat and vegetables, smothered with gravy and eaten with the fingers. The Earl's sandwiches were a bit more refined. As an inveterate gambler obsessed with card playing, he found eating an inconvenience. So he created a portable, utensil-free meal, which would keep his card-playing hands grease-free. These creations soon took on his name.

Whether you like your sandwiches hot or cold, open-faced or closed, a good creation starts with good bread. Team strong-flavored meats, like pastrami, sausages and hams with whole-grain, sourdough, rye, herb, cheese or pumpernickel breads; and pair fruit-flavored and sweet breads, like raisin, limpa, Russian rye, with nuts, fruits, cheese salads, or smoked meat or fish. Try the following in combination:

• apples and Cheddar
• apples and Swiss cheese spreads
• smoked salmon and goat cheese
• prosciutto, figs and Gorgonzola
• beef tenderloin and blue cheese
• ham and Brie
• turkey, avocado and Colby
• bacon, chilies and Cheddar

Be creative with Wisconsin's great variety of cheese—these are just some possibilities: havarti with ham or salami; Camembert with beef, roast pork or smoked turkey; herbed Brie with spicy corned beef; Limburger or Muenster with ham; goat cheese with mild meatloaves or mortadella (an Italian bologna).

Try adding herbs—dill, tarragon, thyme, rosemary—to prepared mustards: use a tablespoon of minced fresh or a teaspoon of dried herbs to one cup Dijon or Dusseldorf-style mustard. Experiment with making your own mayonnaise, or add herbs, flavored vinegars and mustards to store-bought varieties.

The open-faced reuben, a different twist on an easy-to-make classic.

HOT ITALIAN SAUSAGE ROLLS

This sandwich is wonderful with a glass of red wine and a piquant, olive-celery salad.

6 Italian sausages (hot or mild)

1 or 2 large onions, thinly sliced

olive oil

½ cup roasted red pepper, cut in strips

6 large hard rolls

1½ cups ricotta cheese

6 ounces mozzarella cheese, sliced

Cook sausages in a skillet or grill until well browned. Remove, cut in half lengthwise and set aside. Sauté onions in same skillet in 1–2 tablespoons olive oil until they become soft and begin to brown. Remove from heat and mix in red peppers.

Cut rolls in half. Brush a small amount of oil on each side. Arrange both halves of a sausage on each. Distribute the ricotta cheese, the onion-pepper mixture, and the mozzarella evenly over each. Wrap well in foil. Heat at 400 degrees for 10 minutes or until cheese is melted. Serve at once.

Serves 6

REUBEN SANDWICH

An easy to make classic with unique flavors of corned beef, sauerkraut and Swiss cheese.

4 slices of rye bread, toasted lightly

butter, softened

Russian dressing

¾ pounds cooked corned beef, thinly sliced

½ pound thoroughly drained, good quality sauerkraut

4 large slices Swiss cheese, approximately same size as bread

Butter bread on one side generously, spread with Russian dressing. Arrange corned beef over dressing. Top corned beef with sauerkraut and cheese. Place sandwich on baking sheet. Bake in preheated 400 degree oven 5 to 7 minutes until sandwiches are heated through and cheese begins to melt. Place sandwiches under broiler for 1 or 2 minutes to brown cheese lightly. Cut in half, serve with kosher dill pickles.

RUSSIAN DRESSING

1 large whole egg or 3 egg yolks at room temperature

1 teaspoon Dijon mustard

3 teaspoons vinegar or lemon juice

1 to 1½ cups oil (vegetable or combination vegetable and olive oil)

¼ cup ketchup

1½ tablespoons grated horseradish

1 teaspoon grated onion

Worcestershire sauce

salt and pepper

Place egg, mustard and vinegar in a blender or food processor. Whirl until well blended. With blender on, add oil in a very slow and steady stream until the mayonnaise softens, but holds its shape when lifted in a spoon. If too thick, add additional vinegar, lemon juice, or warm water.

Stir ketchup, horseradish and onion into prepared mayonnaise and add Worcestershire sauce to taste, salt, and pepper to taste.

Makes 4 open-faced sandwiches

VEGETARIAN DELIGHT

A healthy, colorful open-faced creation that's great for lunches. Make extra guacamole for snacking.

½ cup Guacamole

4 slices light rye bread, lightly toasted

1 very large tomato thinly sliced, or two small tomatoes, thinly sliced

1 large avocado, peeled and thinly sliced

4 slices Monterey Jack cheese, ⅛-inch thick

½ cup alfalfa sprouts

Spread guacamole evenly over the toasted bread, cover completely with tomato slices, then avocado slices and cheese. Place on a cookie sheet and broil until the cheese is barely melted. Add alfalfa sprouts to each sandwich and serve immediately.

GUACAMOLE

1 large ripe avocado

1 to 2 tablespoons fresh lemon or lime juice

½ to 1 tablespoon chopped fresh coriander (cilantro) or ½ teaspoon ground

1 to 2 canned green chiles (rinsed, seeded, and chopped) and/or cayenne, liquid hot-pepper seasoning, or minced hot green chiles

salt and freshly ground pepper

Cut avocado in half, remove pit, and scoop out pulp with a spoon; or peel. Mash pulp coarsely with a fork while blending in lemon or lime juice or purée in a food processor. Add coriander, chopped chiles, cayenne, or hot-pepper seasoning and salt to taste.

Makes 4 open-faced sandwiches

GRILLED HERO WITH BLEU CHEESE

This is a variation on a popular sandwich with many names: Sub, Hero, Dagwood, Grinder, Poor Boy . . .

2 tablespoons butter

2 tablespoons bleu cheese

8 slices rye or pumpernickel

½ pound sliced turkey

4 ounces Genoa salami, sliced paper thin

melted butter or oil

Cream butter and bleu cheese. Spread on all slices of bread. Divide the turkey and salami evenly over four slices of bread. Cover each with remaining bread, buttered side down. Brush outside of the sandwiches with melted butter or oil and place on grill or skillet. Grill over low heat slowly until nicely browned. Turn over and repeat. Remove, cut in half diagonally, and serve immediately with marinated vegetables.

Serves 4

HOT CRAB AND SHRIMP CROISSANTS

An elegant filling for croissants or puff pastry. Use mini-croissants for appetizers, large croissants for lunch or add a soup and salad for a light dinner.

4 large croissants

4 tablespoons melted unsalted butter

3 tablespoons shallots, minced

2 cups mushrooms, thinly sliced

3 tablespoons fresh lemon juice

1 teaspoon Dijon mustard

1 tablespoon flour

1 cup half and half

1 cup cooked crab meat, thawed if frozen (substitute scallops or combination other fish, chopped)

1 cup cooked shrimp, chopped

2 tablespoons dry Marsala

½ teaspoon lemon rind, grated

2 tablespoons fresh parsley, minced

⅓ cup Parmesan cheese, freshly grated

2 tablespoons vermouth or dry white wine

½ teaspoon dry tarragon

dash of cayenne

salt and freshly grated pepper

grated Parmesan

Cut top third off croissants and scoop out centers, leaving about a ¼-inch shell. Brush insides and tops with 2 tablespoons butter and bake croissant tops, crust side down, on baking sheet in preheated 425 degree oven for 4 to 5 minutes or until golden. In sauce pan, add remaining butter and shallots. Cook over moderately high heat 1 minute, toss mushrooms in the lemon juice, add to shallots along with mustard, continue to cook and stir another 3 minutes. Add flour, reduce heat to a moderate low and cook mixture while stirring for 3 minutes. Whisk in half and half slowly, bring mixture to a boil while whisking and simmer for 5 minutes. Stir in crab meat, shrimp, Marsala, lemon rind, parsley, Parmesan, vermouth, tarragon and cayenne. Cook for an additional 2 or 3 minutes. Adjust seasonings, add salt and pepper to taste. Fill croissants with seafood mixture, sprinkle with additional Parmesan cheese and place under a preheated broiler about 10 inches from heat for about 30 seconds, or until lightly browned. Place tops on croissants and serve.

Makes 4 large croissants

COOKIES FOR EVERYONE

While nearly every family and every ethnic group has its own holiday baking tradition, there's something to be said for going international—especially when it comes to cookies. What better way to enjoy Wisconsin's ethnic past than with these recipes brought by the state's early settlers.

Wisconsin's largest ethnic population, the Germans, begin their holiday season on December 6 with Kriss Kringle or St. Nicholas Day, and end it January 6 on Epiphany. During that period they serve up plateful after plateful of freshly baked cookies. Prominent in German holiday cooking is marzipan, a sweet, rich, ground almond mixture used as a filling for cookies and pastries, and as a candy shaped into miniature fruits or vegetables. Several popular cookies, such as anise-flavored Springerle and spicy Lebkuchen, are best when stored in air-tight containers or tins and allowed to mellow for several weeks.

Common to Wisconsin's Italian families are cookies and breads made with candied fruit that has been laced with Marsala or other sweet dessert wines. Florentine cookies are a favorite example. Deep-fried pastries (Dolci), often made with lemon and a delicate hint of sweet wine, brandy or rum, are also popular.

Appreciated across the state are the cookies of the Scandinavians: the Finnish near Hurley, Norwegians near Stoughton and Mt. Horeb, and the Swedish of the northwest. The Finns are partial to rich butter cookies, often made with cardamon, an orange-clove tasting spice. Swedes and Norwegians enjoy crisp cookies, buttery but not crumbly, and accompanied by their favorite drink, strong coffee. It is a Scandinavian custom that the spirit of Christmas must not leave the house, and so that the spell isn't broken, all holiday visitors must have a tidbit, or cookie, to eat.

The Cornish population, which came to the lead mining region of southwestern Wisconsin in the 1830s, brought along their recipes for holiday tea biscuits and shortbreads redolent with seeds (sesame, caraway, or coriander), and other cookies spiced with saffron and made with syrup in the English tradition.

Ethnic Christmas cookies (clockwise from center tin) florentines, engadiner nusstorte, fattigmands, pepparkakor, brandy snaps and mordegspinnar.

SWEDISH PEPPARKAKOR
(Gingersnaps)

The tangy fragrance of these cookies is part of the wonderful smell of the Swedish Christmas. They should be rolled as thin as parchment.

1½ cups flour

1 teaspoon baking soda

1½ teaspoons ginger

1 teaspoon cinnamon

¼ teaspoon cloves

½ cup butter

¾ cup sugar

1 egg, well beaten

1½ teaspoons dark corn syrup

Sift together dry ingredients and set aside. Cream butter until soft, gradually add sugar, beating thoroughly after each addition. Add egg and corn syrup. Gradually add dry ingredients, mixing well. Chill several hours before rolling. Remove some of the chilled dough, place on lightly floured surface and roll $\frac{1}{16}$-inch thick. Cut with lightly floured cookie cutter into various shapes. Bake at 375 degrees for 6–8 minutes. Remove to cooling rack. After thoroughly cooled, decorate with white icing, if desired.

Makes 4–5 dozen

NORWEGIAN FATTIGMANDS

This bowknot-shaped fried cookie, also referred to as "Poor Man's Cookie," is a traditional holiday treat for Norwegians.

8 egg yolks

½ cup sugar

5 tablespoons melted butter

½ cup sweet cream

2 tablespoons brandy

1 teaspoon ground cardamon

4 egg whites, stiffly beaten

4 cups flour

lard or vegetable shortening

powdered sugar

Beat first 6 ingredients together. Blend in egg whites and flour, and mix well. Chill several hours or overnight. Roll dough thin, ⅛-inch thick. Cut into 5″×2″ dia-mond shapes. Make lengthwise slit in center, pull one corner through it, and tuck it back under itself. Deep fry in lard or shortening only as many cookies as will float uncrowded in one layer. Fry 11 minutes or until golden brown, turning once. Drain on paper towels. While warm, sprinkle with powdered sugar. Store in air-tight containers.

Makes 6 dozen

POLISH CIASTKA Z KONSERWA
(Tea Cakes)

These little Polish tea cakes are special treats served during the holiday season.

½ cup butter

½ cup sugar

1 egg yolk, slightly beaten

2 egg whites

1 cup flour

½ teaspoon salt

½ teaspoon vanilla

½ cup or more finely chopped nuts

¼ cup preserves (apricot, currant, raspberry, etc.)

Sift together flour and salt and set aside. Cream butter and sugar until light. Add egg yolk and mix well. Gradually add flour mixture, mixing well after each addition. Roll into small balls. Dip into unbeaten egg whites and roll in chopped nuts. Place on buttered baking sheets, and press down centers with finger or thimble. Bake in 325-degree oven for 5 minutes. Remove and press centers again, and return to oven for about 10–15 minutes or until golden. Remove from oven and while warm, fill indentations with preserves.

Makes 4 dozen

FINNISH MORDEGSPINNAR

These holiday cookies are also referred to as "Finnish Coffee Fingers."

1 cup butter

1 teaspoon almond extract

½ cup sugar

1½ cups sifted flour

½ cup blanched almonds, finely chopped

3 tablespoons sugar

2 egg whites, beaten lightly

Cream butter and almond extract together, gradually add sugar, creaming until fluffy and light. Add flour in fourths, thoroughly blending after each addition. Chill in refrigerator several hours. Combine almonds and 3 tablespoons sugar and set aside. Pinch off small pieces of dough and with lightly floured hands, roll into log shapes about the thickness of your little finger, 2–3 inches long. Brush with egg white and roll in almond mixture. Carefully place on cookie sheet. Bend into crescent shapes, if desired. Bake at 350 degrees for 10–12 minutes or until golden.

Makes 5 dozen

ITALIAN FLORENTINES

This is an elegant Italian cookie that is wonderful with fruit or ice cream.

¾ cup heavy cream

¼ cup sugar

¼ cup flour

½ cup blanched almonds, very finely chopped

½ pound candied orange peel, finely chopped

8 ounces sweet chocolate

Stir cream and sugar together until well blended. Stir in flour, almonds and orange peel. Drop dough by scant teaspoonfuls on heavily greased and floured baking sheet. Flatten cookie with spoon. Bake 10–12 minutes or until just lightly brown around edges. Leave on cookie sheet for few minutes to firm up. Melt chocolate over hot water. Turn cookies upside down, spread with chocolate and if desired, make swirl pattern with fork tines. Allow to dry several hours or overnight at room temperature until chocolate is firm. Store in covered container or in refrigerator.

Makes 5 dozen

CORNISH BRANDY SNAPS

These Cornish cookies take some practice in the beginning, so don't be discouraged with a less than perfect first effort.

½ cup sugar

6 tablespoons butter

1 cup flour

8½ tablespoons imported English golden syrup, or substitute 6 tablespoons light corn syrup with 1¼ tablespoons molasses

1 teaspoon ground ginger

2 teaspoons brandy

Cornish Clotted Cream

Melt syrup, butter and sugar over pan of hot water. Sift together flour and ground ginger, and add these. Mix in brandy. Thoroughly grease baking tray, and put teaspoonfuls of mixture onto tray, allowing each to spread widely. Bake at 350 degrees until a nice brown. Cool a moment and wrap each brandy snap around handle of well greased wooden spoon. Biscuits stiffen quickly, so speed is essential. If necessary put them back in oven for a few moments to soften. (If cookies cool too much, they harden and are difficult to shape.) When rolled, allow to cool and harden, then fill with Cornish Clotted Cream when ready to serve.

CORNISH CLOTTED CREAM
2 cups very fresh milk

½ cup sugar

2 tablespoons brandy

Choose wide, shallow earthenware pan. Combine milk, sugar and brandy and let stand out overnight in summer or for 24 hours in cold weather. Then slowly, without simmering, raise temperature of milk over low heat until solid ring starts to form around the edge. Without shaking pan, very carefully remove it from heat and leave overnight or a little longer in a cool place. Thick crust of cream can then be skimmed off surface with large spoon. If you don't have time to make traditional clotted cream, make this substitute for it:

1½ cups heavy cream

½ cup confectioners' sugar

2 tablespoons brandy

Just before serving, beat cream in chilled bowl with whisk or electric beater until it thickens slightly. Add ½ cup of sugar, and continue to beat until cream forms stiff peaks. With rubber spatula gently but thoroughly fold in brandy. Fill pastry bag with brandied cream and pipe into the brandy snaps. Serve at once.

Makes 4½ dozen

ENGLISH TEA BISCUITS

This 1855 cookie recipe dates back to Bridget Mulhairn, mother of Maria Shaw and great-grandmother of Mary Brodzeller of Madison.

6 cups flour

4 teaspoons baking powder

1 teaspoon salt

2 cups sugar

1 teaspoon nutmeg

1½ cups currants

grated rind of 1 lemon

1¼ cups sour milk—with 1 teaspoon soda added

1 cup bacon drippings

2 or more cups of sugar for rolling cookies

In small bowl add currants to 1 cup of hot water. Let sit 15 minutes. Drain and set aside. In large bowl mix flour, baking powder, sugar, salt and nutmeg. Add plumped currants and lemon rind. Add bacon drippings and blend well. Add milk a little at a time and blend. Handle dough as little as possible so as not to toughen. Pat dough, a small portion at a time, into balls. Grease cookie sheets well. In saucer place ½ cup sugar. Roll cookie ball in sugar and flatten with glass onto cookie sheet. Bake at 350 degrees 12–15 minutes until bottoms are an attractive brown.

Makes 10 dozen

SWISS ENGADINER NUSSTORTE

These German bar cookies are wonderful keepers. Like *leckerli* they improve and mellow with age.

CRUST
1 cup butter, room temperature

1 cup sugar

1 tablespoon rum

2 eggs

⅛ teaspoon salt

4 cups flour

1 lemon, grated

Place all ingredients in bowl and work with fingers or pastry blender until all particles combine to form dough. Smear dough on lightly floured surface to make sure butter is well incorporated. Divide dough in half; roll each between sheets of wax paper to make rectangle about 9″×13″. Chill.

FILLING
1⅓ cups sugar

3 tablespoons water

1 cup heavy cream, heated

1 lemon grated

3 tablespoons honey

3 cups walnuts, chopped coarsely

egg wash (1 egg yolk and 1 tablespoon cream)

Cook sugar with water over low heat in large heavy skillet or saucepan until it liquefies and becomes light golden brown. Gently stir in hot cream. Stir over low heat until sugar blends with cream. Scrape bottom of pan with small whisk to loosen sugar syrup. Stir in lemon and honey, and fold in nuts. Cool thoroughly.

ASSEMBLY
Fit half of dough in bottom of 9″×13″ pan and chill 15–20 minutes. Spread cooled filling evenly onto dough-lined pan. Cut remaining dough into ½-inch strips. Move these fragile strips carefully. Place them in a lattice pattern over top. Brush with egg wash and place on bottom shelf of preheated 350-degree oven for 45 minutes. Remove and cool on racks; cut into small squares. Store for weeks in airtight container.

Makes 3 dozen

Home-baked holiday traditions
from around the world

CLASSIC BREADS

Stollens, striezels, kringles, houskas—holiday breads in any nationality are a wonderful addition to the season's festivities. During this time so rich in traditions, bread-making takes on new prominence. In many families, favored recipes have been passed down through generations, an important link to their ethnic heritage. In Wisconsin, with our broad mix of ethnic groups, the holidays will bring loaves, cakes and buns of every shape, texture and aroma.

For some nationalities, the holiday celebrating and bread-making begins with the start of Advent. German stollen, a rich heavy cake that keeps for weeks, is traditionally served from Advent Sunday through the Christmas season. A loaf-shaped cake, it originated in Dresden nearly three hundred years ago and is said to symbolize the Christ child in swaddling clothes.

In Sweden December 13 marks the appearance of St. Lucia, the Queen of Light, and bearer of Lucia Buns. She is customarily represented by a young girl, daughter, relative or friend of the family, dressed in white and wearing a lighted crown on her head. Singing the Lucia song, she bears bread and coffee to the bedrooms in the household early in the morning.

It is said to be the custom of children in Milan to leave Panettone bread and a bowl of water on New Year's Eve for the camels of the bearers of gifts to the Christ child. And in Greece the feast of St. Basil is celebrated on January 1, with the breaking of bread. Known as New Year's Bread or St. Basil Bread, it accompanies a gift giving ceremony and honors the great philanthropist who reportedly developed an entire city for the needy.

Steeped in tradition, holiday breads feed both the body and soul. Here are just a few classics to spark your holiday baking.

Golden saffron St. Lucia buns (center) are surrounded by (clockwise from top) fruit-filled panettones, almond kringle, hearty stollen, sugar-dusted potica and aromatic New Year's Day bread.

ALMOND KRINGLE

A wonderfully rich Danish pastry that you'll want to make year around.

1 envelope (¼ ounce) active dry yeast
⅓ cup warm milk
1 tablespoon sugar
3 egg yolks, slightly beaten
¾ cup whipping cream
3½ cups all-purpose flour
¼ cup sugar
1 teaspoon salt
½ cup butter, chilled
1 recipe Almond Filling
¼ cup pearl sugar, or coarsely crushed sugar cubes
1 egg white, slightly beaten
¼ cup sliced almonds

In a small bowl combine the yeast, milk, 1 tablespoon sugar, egg yolks and cream; let stand ten minutes. In a large bowl blend flour, ¼ cup sugar and salt. With a pastry blender cut in butter until pieces are the size of kidney beans. Add yeast mixture slowly, folding in only until dry ingredients are moistened. Turn dough out onto a slightly floured board, dust with flour and knead 4 or 5 times. Place in clean bowl, cover and refrigerate 12 to 24 hours. (This will not rise.)

Prepare Almond Filling (see below) and set aside.

With a rolling pin, pound dough until smooth and ¾-inch thick. Roll dough into a 15×30-inch rectangle and spread filling to within 1 inch of edges. Roll up tightly, in a jelly roll fashion. Sprinkle work surface with pearl sugar, roll dough in sugar, brush surface with egg white and roll in sugar a second time.

Lay rolled dough on a greased baking sheet. Shape it into a large pretzel by curving like a "U," then looping each end around the opposite side about 5 inches from the ends. Tuck ends under. Again brush with egg white, and sprinkle with almonds. Cover and let rise in a warm place for 40 minutes. Bake in preheated oven, 375 degrees, for 25–30 minutes or until golden brown.

ALMOND FILLING

1 package (8 ounces) almond paste
¾ cup chopped almonds
½ cup sugar
1 egg white
1 teaspoon ground cinnamon
1½ teaspoons almond extract

Break almond paste into pieces. With a mixer, combine all ingredients.

Serves 12

PANETTONE

Decorate this festive Italian bread with candied cherries and a thin glaze of powdered sugar and rum or sherry.

⅓ cup each candied citron, golden raisins, dark raisins, mixed candied fruit and halved cherries
¼ cup Marsala wine, sherry or rum
⅓ cup sugar
⅔ cup butter
¼ cup milk
2 packages dry yeast
½ cup water (105–110 degrees)
3–3¾ cups flour
½ teaspoon salt
1 teaspoon anise seeds, crushed
1 teaspoon grated lemon peel
1 teaspoon vanilla
2 eggs
2 egg yolks
¼ cup pine nuts or slivered almonds

Soak fruit in liquor for 30–60 minutes. In a saucepan place sugar, butter and milk. Heat until butter melts; cool to lukewarm.

Proof yeast with a dash of sugar and water. Place proofed yeast in electric mixer bowl, add cooled milk mixture, flour, salt, anise seeds, lemon peel and vanilla. Mix well, then add eggs and egg yolks one at a time, beating well after each addition. Mix in fruit, liquor and nuts. Turn out onto floured surface and knead until smooth and elastic. Add more flour if dough is too sticky. Place in a lightly greased bowl, turn to coat and let rise in a draft-free, warm place until double in size (1–2 hours).

Punch down dough and place in greased pans—either one 3-pound coffee can or three 1-pound cans. Let rise 1 hour. Bake at 350 degrees for 40 minutes or until golden to dark brown. Cool on racks.

Makes 1 large or 3 small loaves

GERMAN STOLLEN

This recipe makes two large oval loaves or four smaller ones—perfect for gift-giving. As a leftover, slice and lightly toast and serve with hot, strong black coffee.

1½ cups mixed candied fruit
½ cup candied cherries, halved
½ cup golden raisins
½ cup currants
3 tablespoons rum, brandy or bourbon
2 sticks butter
½ cup sugar
¾ cup milk
2 packages dry yeast
½ cup water (110 degrees)
5½–6 cups flour
½ teaspoon salt
5 cardamon pods (seeds removed and crushed)
¼ teaspoon mace
3 eggs
½ cup lightly toasted slivered almonds
½ teaspoon almond extract
½ teaspoon vanilla extract
grated peel from 1 orange
melted butter

Mix candied fruit, cherries, raisins and currants in a bowl with the liquor. Set aside 30–60 minutes. Place butter, sugar and milk in a saucepan and heat until butter melts. Set aside to cool slightly. Proof yeast in a glass bowl with ½ teaspoon sugar and water until it foams.

Place flour, salt, cardamon and mace in electric mixer bowl. Add yeast and cooled milk mixture. Stir. Add eggs one at a time and blend well after each. Add fruit with liquor, almonds, flavorings and grated orange peel. Blend well. Turn onto a lightly floured board and knead until smooth and elastic, 5–10 minutes.

Place in oiled bowl, turn to coat, cover and let rise in a warm, draft-free place until double in size, 1½–2 hours. Punch down and divide. Pat into ovals. Brush with melted butter and make a crease slightly off-center. Fold so edges do not touch. Brush with more melted butter. Bake at 425 degrees for 35–40 minutes or until golden brown and tests done. Cool and sprinkle with powdered sugar.

Makes 2 large or 4 small loaves

NEW YEAR'S DAY SWEET BREAD

This Greek bread is served for the feast of St. Basil.

2 packages dry yeast

1 cup warm water

1 teaspoon sugar

5½–6 cups flour

1 teaspoon salt

1 teaspoon cinnamon

¼ teaspoon nutmeg

¼ teaspoon cloves

4 large eggs

¾ cup sugar

½ cup butter, melted

1 beaten egg

1 tablespoon water

½ teaspoon sugar

½ teaspoon vanilla

sesame seeds or sliced almonds

Mix together the yeast, warm water and 1 teaspoon sugar in a small bowl. Set aside to activate for 5 minutes. In a large bowl combine 3 cups of the flour with the salt, cinnamon, nutmeg and cloves. Make a well in the center of the dry ingredients and add the yeast mixture. Stir in some of the remaining flour.

Beat eggs and sugar together, add the melted butter and mix well. Add to flour mixture, mixing well until all the flour in the bowl has been incorporated. Add 2 cups of flour and continue to mix with a spoon. Add remaining ½ cup flour and mix by hand. Dough will become smooth and non-sticky. Pat flour on top of dough and gather from sides of bowl to shape into a ball. Cover and allow to rise 45 minutes in a warm place.

Punch down the dough and turn onto a floured surface. Roll into a 9 × 12-inch rectangle and cut into 3 equal strips, lengthwise. Braid the strips beginning at the midpoint, braiding down the lower half and then up to the top. Pinch each end tightly and bring ends together, placing one over the other and tucking it under the braid to form a circle. It will be about 10 inches around. Place on a round pizza pan or baking sheet large enough to allow for rising. In a small bowl combine the egg, water, sugar and vanilla. Brush mixture on the dough and sprinkle with sesame seeds or almonds. Let rise for 30 minutes in warm area.

Bake in preheated oven at 350 degrees for 15 minutes. Reduce heat to 300 degrees and bake 25 minutes more. Allow to cool on pan for 5 minutes.

Makes 1 large braid

POTICA

No Yugoslavian holiday's complete without this moist, flavorful yeast bread.

1½ cups warm milk

¾ cup butter

½ cup sugar

2 packages dry yeast

½ cup warm water

1 teaspoon salt

2 teaspoons grated lemon peel

2 eggs

6½–7 cups flour

Place milk, butter and sugar in a saucepan and heat until butter melts. Remove and cool to lukewarm. Proof yeast with water and a dash of sugar until foamy.

Place proofed yeast, milk mixture, salt, lemon peel, and eggs in an electric mixer bowl and blend well. Beat in flour, 1 cup at a time. Place in a greased bowl, turn and let rise in a warm, draft-free area until doubled, 1–1½ hours.

Punch down and roll dough into a 20 × 15-inch rectangle (or 2 of smaller size). Spread filling (see below) to within 1 inch of the edges. Roll as a jelly roll and place on a greased cookie sheet, spiraling into a tight rope shape. Let rise, covered, 30–60 minutes until double in size. Bake at 350 degrees for 45 minutes. Cool and sprinkle with powdered sugar.

WALNUT FILLING

3 cups (¾ pound) walnuts, ground

⅓ cup half and half

¼ cup sugar

2 teaspoons cinnamon

1 tablespoon vanilla

⅓ cup honey

1 egg, separated

½ teaspoon grated lemon peel

Bring half and half to a simmer. Stir in nuts, sugar, cinnamon, lemon peel, vanilla, honey and egg yolk. Beat egg white with a wire whisk and fold into nut mixture.

Makes 1 large or 2 small ropes

ST. LUCIA BUNS

In traditional Swedish households, these saffron buns are served on December 13.

1 envelope (¼ ounce) active dry yeast

¼ cup warm water

¾ cup milk

1 teaspoon saffron threads or ¹⁄₁₆ teaspoon powdered saffron

½ cup butter

½ cup sugar

1 teaspoon salt

grated rind of 1 orange

⅔ cup golden raisins

2 eggs, slightly beaten

3½–4 cups bread flour

1 beaten egg

½ cup currants or raisins

In a small bowl, stir yeast into warm water and let stand 5 minutes. Combine milk and saffron in small saucepan. Bring to a boil over medium heat, stirring until milk turns a deep yellow. (If using saffron threads, strain.) Pour milk into a large bowl, stir in butter, sugar, salt, orange rind and golden raisins. Cool slightly. Stir in yeast mixture and eggs. Beat to keep mixture smooth and stir in enough flour to make a stiff dough.

Turn onto a lightly floured board. Cover with a dry cloth; let stand 5–15 minutes. Grease a large bowl and set it aside. Knead dough until smooth, about 10 minutes. Place in greased bowl, turning to grease all sides. Cover and let rise in a warm place until double in bulk, about 2 hours.

Punch down dough and roll out to a ¾-inch thickness. Cut into 8-inch strips and form into a variety of shapes, decorating with currants or raisins. Place buns on greased baking sheets, cover and let rise until double in bulk, about 1 hour. Brush with beaten egg and bake in preheated oven, 375 degrees, for 15–20 minutes. Do not overbake.

Makes 20–24 buns

AUTHORS &
PHOTOGRAPHER

Authors **SUZANNE BRECKENRIDGE** (left) and **MARGE SNYDER** (right) began their "Country Gourmet" food column in *Wisconsin Trails* magazine in 1981, shortly after their fame had spread as Madison-based cooking instructors.

They made their cooking debut at an herb growing class they were enrolled in, and were soon conducting cooking classes in Marge's kitchen. As word of their knowledge about food and their passion for sharing the joys of cooking spread, they outgrew the kitchen and moved their popular "Herb Forum" classes to a Madison cooking wares specialty shop. They have, in the past, catered together, written a weekly newspaper column, taken their classes on the road, and sponsored public forums in which area chefs demonstrate their specialties.

Both draw on prior skills and education in their work as "Country Gourmets" —Suzanne, who also operates a flourishing business as a caterer and as a food stylist (including the food styling for "Country Gourmet"), has a Master of Fine Arts degree from the University of Wisconsin–Madison and has worked as a graphic designer. Marge, with a Bachelor of Arts degree in English from Bradley, is a former English teacher and director of the regional Herb Society. Both authors live in Madison with their families.

A Madison-based commercial photographer for fifteen years, **JOE PASKUS** travels extensively for his corporate clients, shooting architectural and a wide variety of other subjects for annual reports. Trained in architecture at the University of Illinois, Joe got his start in photography when he submitted winning photographs for a project to his employing architectural firm. Known for a strong sense of design and orderly form,

his photographic style draws on this background.

Joe, who lives in Madison with his family, has been the food photographer for "Country Gourmet" since its inception. "It's my most enjoyable shoot," he says, "especially at the end, when it's time for another of Marge and Suzanne's incredible feasts."

LONG GREEN

JOE PASKUS

INDEX